Collins

11+ Verbal Reasoning

Quick Practice Tests
Ages 10-11
Book 2

Shelley Welsh

Contents

About this book

Familiarisation with 11+ test-style questions is a critical step in preparing your child for the 11+ selection tests. This book gives children lots of opportunities to test themselves in short, manageable bursts, helping to build confidence and improve the chance of test success.

It contains 60 tests designed to develop key verbal reasoning skills.

- Each test is designed to be completed within a short amount of time. Frequent, short bursts of revision are found to be more productive than lengthier sessions.

- GL Assessment tests can be quite time-pressured so these practice tests will help your child become accustomed to this style of questioning.

- We recommend your child uses a pencil to complete the tests, so that they can rub out the answers and try again later.

- Children will need a pencil and a rubber to complete the tests as well as some spare paper for rough working. They will also need to be able to see a clock/watch and should have a quiet place in which to do the tests.

- Your child should **not** use a calculator for any of these tests.

- Answers to each question are provided at the back of the book, with explanations given where appropriate.

- After completing the tests, children should revisit their weaker areas and attempt to improve their scores and timings.

Synonyms

You have 6 minutes to complete this test.

You have 10 questions to complete within the time given.

In each question, underline the two words (one from each group) that are most similar in meaning.

EXAMPLE

(<u>champion</u>   plaque   loser)

(leader   trophy   <u>winner</u>)

① (squander   profit   create)

(bank   waste   increase)

② (edit   limit   publish)

(restrict   finish   source)

③ (rinse   cascade   soak)

(stream   drip   waterfall)

④ (burgle   police   prison)

(crime   scene   steal)

⑤ (illiterate   insufferable   unlawful)

(illicit   ignorant   illegible)

⑥ (succumb   disagree   digress)

(attempt   conquer   surrender)

⑦ (deter   prevent   deflect)

(divert   attract   deny)

⑧ (display   shroud   curtain)

(draw   shred   covering)

⑨ (phoney   repetitive   imaginary)

(audio   authentic   fake)

⑩ (miserly   sparse   plentiful)

(scarce   humble   sly)

Score: .... / 10

In each question, underline the two words (one from each group) that are most opposite in meaning.

EXAMPLE

(<u>plentiful</u>   mediocre   intermittent)

(ample   <u>scarce</u>   some)

---

1 (fragile   determined   timely)

(slight   arid   robust)

6 (wretched   frantic   lavish)

(grand   meagre   exciting)

2 (vulnerable   indifferent   resilient)

(concerned   able   opposite)

7 (valiant   tranquil   cautious)

(brave   tender   cowardly)

3 (chaotic   furious   interminable)

(angry   endless   controlled)

8 (arrogant   virtuous   simple)

(corrupt   moral   astute)

4 (calculating   insistent   inhibited)

(spontaneous   kindred   inadequate)

9 (surplus   serious   insignificant)

(deficiency   extra   wholesome)

5 (jubilant   disgruntled   frivolous)

(heavy   unfriendly   sad)

10 (brisk   amiable   scrupulous)

(precise   slapdash   pristine)

Score: .... / 10

Word Combinations

You have 6 minutes to complete this test.

You have 10 questions to complete within the time given.

In each question, combine one word from the first group with one word from the second group to create one new word.

The word from the first group always comes first.

Underline the correct word from each group and write in the new word.

EXAMPLE

(clock <u>card</u> car)

(<u>board</u> hand ring)   ....*cardboard*....

---

(1) (fore bee hand)
(hind ground full)   ....

(2) (ball flood awe)
(gates court sum)   ....

(3) (ant mis con)
(stake elope tack)   ....

(4) (ware face be)
(house warned front)   ....

(5) (for finger nail)
(tip head brow)   ....

(6) (file paper news)
(book agent staple)   ....

(7) (hand none any)
(few those some)   ....

(8) (day how moose)
(stash ever about)   ....

(9) (slide below under)
(paint fly line)   ....

(10) (normal adapt cape)
(able cloak eyes)   ....

Score: .... / 10

Complete the Third Pair the Same Way

You have 6 minutes to complete this test.

You have 10 questions to complete within the time given.

Find the word that completes the third pair of words so that it follows the same pattern as the first two pairs.

EXAMPLE

teams seam   fails sail   lands ....**sand**........

(Replace the first letter with the last letter.)

1.   bank bunk   sank sunk   flank ....

2.   bling cling   mine nine   fun ....

3.   foster rest   panted dent   hasten ....

4.   plaster peas   centre cent   minute ....

5.   start tar   scalp pal   crop ....

6.   bandage and   mustard star   thoroughly ....

7.   define find   mother them   posted ....

8.   camper came   world word   solder ....

9.   cancel can   banter tan   create ....

10.   fling sling   chard shard   coil ....

Score: .... / 10

You have 6 minutes to complete this test.

You have 10 questions to complete within the time given.

In each question, three letters have been removed from the word in capitals.

These three letters correctly spell a new word without changing their order.

Write in the three missing letters.

EXAMPLE

Pilar is **PING** carrots for our vegetable soup. ...... **EEL** ......

(The word in capitals is PEELING.)

(1) Today, my grandmother opened her new retail **BUESS**. ....

(2) The fire, **IGED** by the bomb blast, raged for hours. ....

(3) A prisoner has allegedly **ESED** from the high-security wing. ....

(4) Mia has **INITED** her grandmother's green eyes. ....

(5) When Mum lost her job, our **CIRCUMSCES** changed immediately. ....

(6) Yolanda carried the **DLE** of firewood to the campfire. ....

(7) It was **APPNT** that Boris hadn't revised for the maths test. ....

(8) Billie opened the door to find a **STGE** woman standing in the rain. ....

(9) The cat lay by the fire, purring **CONTEDLY**. ....

(10) The astronomer studied the Moon's **CERS** through the telescope. ....

Score: .... / 10

8

Test	Code Pairs
6	You have 8 minutes to complete this test.
	You have 10 questions to complete within the time given.

Use the alphabet below to help you with these questions.

A B C D E F G H I J K L M N O P Q R S T U V W X Y Z

In each question, use the code provided to identify the new word or code.

EXAMPLE

If the code for **BELT** is **DGNV**, what is the code for **MOST**?   <u>OQUV</u>

(*each letter is +2*)

---

(1) If the code for **MOTH** is **LNSG**, what is the code for **WING**?   ....

(2) If the code for **STAR** is **TWBU**, what is the code for **MOON**?   ....

(3) If the code for **TIPS** is **UHQR**, what is **IDMO** the code for?   ....

(4) If the code for **PACKAGE** is **UZGIDDG**, what is the code for **RESIDES**?   ....

(5) If the code for **BLANKET** is **DBVOCHY**, what is the code for **BEDROOM**?   ....

(6) If the code for **STICKY** is **QPCUAM**, what is **DHIOUF** the code for?   ....

(7) If the code for **LIKE** is **ORPL**, what is the code for **FILE**?   ....

(8) If the code for **DINNER** is **HSNVKM**, what is the code for **SUPPER**?   ....

(9) If the code for **WET** is **DXH**, what is the code for **DRY**?   ....

(10) If the code for **SMALL** is **JXSXE**, what is the code for **LARGE**?   ....

Score: .... / 10

Code Sets

You have 6 minutes to complete this test.

You have 9 questions to complete within the time given
(3 sets of codes with 3 questions each).

In each set of questions, three of the four words are given in code. These codes are not in the same order as the words and one code is missing. Use these codes to answer each question and write your answer on the dotted line.

EXAMPLE

TALE	LEAP	PEAT	HELP
1532	6251	4236	

Find the code for the word **HELP**.   .... **4236** ....

PALE	LAME	REAL	RAMP
4351	2341	6134	

(1) Find the code for the word **RAMP**.   ....

(2) Find the code for the word **LAMP**.   ....

(3) Find the word that has the number code **5134**.   ....

FAWN	WAND	FADE	DANE
3142	6125	2145	

(4) Find the code for the word **WAND**.   ....

(5) Find the code for the word **DAWN**.   ....

(6) Find the word that has the number code **2516**.   ....

SEAL	HATE	TEST	TALE
2531	4365	6526	

(7) Find the code for the word **HATE**.   ....

(8) Find the code for the word **TALE**.   ....

(9) Find the word that has the number code **1324**.   ....

Score: .... / 9

Code Sequences

You have 6 minutes to complete this test.

You have 10 questions to complete within the time given.

Use the alphabet below to help you with these questions.

A B C D E F G H I J K L M N O P Q R S T U V W X Y Z

In each question, find the letters that are next in the sequence.

EXAMPLE					
SL	RM	RN	QO	QP	_____PQ_____

(1st letter −1, 0, −1, 0, −1; 2nd letter +1)

①	ST	XP	BM	EK	GJ	....
②	XF	AB	EY	HU	LR	....
③	YC	XA	VZ	SX	OW	....
④	AP	DN	JL	MJ	SH	....
⑤	FL	EM	DQ	CR	BV	....
⑥	NA	OC	PE	QG	RI	....
⑦	BB	ZD	XF	VH	TJ	....
⑧	UR	PM	KH	FC	AX	....
⑨	ID	KV	OP	UL	CJ	....
⑩	CZ	FW	EX	HU	GV	....

Score: .... / 10

Related Words

You have 6 minutes to complete this test.

You have 10 questions to complete within the time given.

In each question, three of the words are related in some way.

Underline the two words that do not relate to the other three.

EXAMPLE

furious   <u>upset</u>   cross   <u>worried</u>   angry

(The underlined words are not synonyms for angry.)

(1) cup   spoon   dish   pan   bowl

(2) horse   mare   vixen   ewe   bull

(3) pick   let   choose   select   permit

(4) rich   aspiring   ambitious   enterprising   successful

(5) apple   orchard   grape   vineyard   allotment

(6) stable   kennel   burrow   barn   nest

(7) ornate   meagre   decorative   beautiful   fancy

(8) hail   snow   sun   wind   rain

(9) mark   tick   blemish   smack   scar

(10) object   subject   aim   topic   purpose

Score: .... / 10

Complete the Sum

In each question, write in the number that correctly completes the sum.

EXAMPLE

5 + 7 = 3 + ...9....

① 13 + 5 = 3 × ....

② 8 × 10 ÷ 20 = ...

③ (6 × 7) + 8 = 2 × ....

④ 45 − 17 = 7 × ....

⑤ (7 × 8) + (12 × 8) = 200 − ....

⑥ 48 ÷ 3 = 25 − ....

⑦ 12^2 + 21 = 120 + ...

⑧ (13 × 2) − 16 = 90 ÷ ....

⑨ (3 × 3 × 3) + (3 × 0) = 9 × ....

⑩ 8^2 − (12 × 3) = (2 × 2 × 2) + (5 × ....)

Score: .... / 10

Word Analogies

In each question, underline the two words (one from each group) that will complete the phrase in the best way.

EXAMPLE

Bird is to

(egg fly beak)

as **snake** is to

(poison slither scales).   (*the words are to do with the movement of the animals*)

---

① **Smell** is to

(scent nose sniff)

as **hear** is to

(ear listen head).

② **Content** is to

(satisfied list items)

as **concerned** is to

(disappointed rational worried).

③ **Car** is to

(wheels exhaust vehicle)

as **ship** is to

(waves vessel mast).

④ **Even** is to

(odd middle equal)

as **rough** is to

(tough sticky smooth).

⑤ **Disagree** is to

(clash disrupt coincide)

as **flounder** is to

(falter succeed freeze).

⑥ **Organ** is to

(key kidney band)

as **violin** is to

(bow string orchestra).

⑦ **Eerie** is to

(eagle mysterious nest)

as **fragile** is to

(brittle frog robust).

⑧ **Rainbow** is to

(childhood colour arc)

as **necklace** is to

(bangle jewel railway).

⑨ **Energetic** is to

(electrical lethargic flashy)

as **productive** is to

(resulting desperate useless).

⑩ **Resolute** is to

(cautious clever determined)

as **exquisite** is to

(tremendous beautiful sensible).

Score: .... / 10

Letter Connections

You have 6 minutes to complete this test.

You have 10 questions to complete within the time given.

In each question, write in the letter that fits into both sets of brackets.

The letter should finish the word before the brackets and start the word after the brackets.

EXAMPLE

ti [.....n.....] est

te [.....n.....] ote   (*The four words are tin, nest, ten and note.*)

① fa [..............] ipe

ca [..............] ent

② se [..............] ar

pa [..............] et

③ loi [..............] ag

bu [..............] il

④ fil [..............] ip

pol [..............] ob

⑤ gri [..............] up

pi [..............] ig

⑥ pa [..............] outh

buo [..............] ap

⑦ spen [..............] ame

gran [..............] aint

⑧ toxi [..............] able

ar [..............] hafe

⑨ fli [..............] ony

tra [..............] ledge

⑩ ke [..............] earn

tra [..............] awn

Score: .... / 10

Hidden Words

In each question, a four-letter word can be found by combining the end (or whole) of one word with the beginning (or whole) of the next word.

Underline the two words that contain these letters and write in the new four-letter word.

EXAMPLE

We <u>left our</u> bags beside the front door. ....**tour**......... (le**ft ou**r)

---

(1) Tom and I got the same answer. ....

(2) Fleur has a basic knowledge of Spanish. ....

(3) The company managers have invested in new laptops. ....

(4) Add chilli peppers to the sauce for extra flavour. ....

(5) We heard a bleating sheep in the farmer's field. ....

(6) Dexter is our cousin but we've only seen him once. ....

(7) The magnificent acrobatic display blew us away! ....

(8) Mum likes to watch the ten o'clock news. ....

(9) I didn't have a bike but neither did Katie. ....

(10) Clio started watching the football at one o'clock. ....

Score: .... / 10

Problem Solving

In each question, read the information provided and then write in your answer.

EXAMPLE

Alf weighs 19 kg more than Callum.

Callum is twice the weight of Ben, who weighs 12 kg.

How much does Alf weigh?   .... 43 kg ....

---

(1) Seb, Stella, Erin, Joe and Ahmed are helping their parents.

All of them apart from Ahmed take out the bins.

Stella and Erin do the washing up.

Ahmed walks the dog.

Everyone apart from Joe and Ahmed brush the floors.

Joe does the dusting and washes up.

Stella walks and feeds the dog.

Who does the fewest tasks?   ....

(2) The kitchen clock is 25 minutes slow and shows a time of 7.55 pm.

What was the correct time 35 minutes ago?   ....

(3) Harry is Carl's mother's brother and Freddy is Carl's father's father.

Robert is Freddy's son.

Who is Carl's grandfather?   ....

(4) Fay is 11 years and 4 months old.

Her brother Guy is 3 years and 8 months older than her.

If Fay was born in April 1998, in which month and year was Guy born?   ....

Questions continue on next page

5) Mo, Ethan and Eve go to at least one after-school club.
Mo is in the hockey club but he didn't join the choir with the others.
Ethan is the only one who doesn't play football.
Eve is in the art club.

Who definitely attends three clubs?

....

6) Ursula's dad bought a new car 2 years ago for £12,546.
He sold it last week for 25% less than he bought it for.

How much money did he lose on the sale?

....

7) Klaus, Petra, Chen, Ivy and Ruby did a sponsored run for charity.
Petra raised three times as much as Chen.
Ruby raised £15 more than Klaus.
Ivy raised half as much as Chen.
The highest amount raised was £80.
Petra raised £75.

How much money did Klaus raise?

....

8) When Carla has her birthday next week, she will be two-and-a-half times older than her cousin, Beth.
Carla's brother, Max, is five years older than Beth.
Max is 15.

How old will Carla be on her birthday next week?

....

Score: .... / 8

Use the alphabet below to help you with these questions.

A B C D E F G H I J K L M N O P Q R S T U V W X Y Z

In each question, write in the letters that will complete the phrase in the best way.

EXAMPLE

FG is to **HI** as **ST** is to .... UV ....

(1st letter +2, 2nd letter +2)

① **XE** is to **BA** as **CR** is to ....

② **QP** is to **PO** as **ML** is to ....

③ **AZ** is to **CX** as **DW** is to ....

④ **DM** is to **BK** as **VR** is to ....

⑤ **ZY** is to **ED** as **WV** is to ....

⑥ **BY** is to **WF** as **EV** is to ....

⑦ **BL** is to **YO** as **JA** is to ....

⑧ **WH** is to **SD** as **VM** is to ....

⑨ **OW** is to **WW** as **KW** is to ....

⑩ **AZ** is to **BW** as **GT** is to ....

Score: .... / 10

Letters for Numbers

You have 6 minutes to complete this test.

You have 10 questions to complete within the time given.

In each question, numbers are shown as letters. Find the answer to the sum and write it in as a **letter**.

EXAMPLE

A = 2   B = 6   C = 10   D = 5   E = 11

What is the answer to this sum **written as a letter**?   C – D + B = ...**E**....   *(10 – 5 + 6 = 11)*

---

(1)   A = 2   B = 7   C = 12   D = 3   E = 18

What is the answer to this sum **written as a letter**?   D × C ÷ A = ...

(2)   A = 12   B = 24   C = 3   D = 5   E = 2

What is the answer to this sum **written as a letter**?   (A × C × E) ÷ C = ...

(3)   A = 4   B = 5   C = 11   D = 26   E = 20

What is the answer to this sum **written as a letter**?   C + E – B = ...

(4)   A = 20   B = 60   C = 5   D = 16   E = 20

What is the answer to this sum **written as a letter**?   (A ÷ C) × E – A = ...

(5)   A = 2   B = 6   C = 10   D = 8   E = 40

What is the answer to this sum **written as a letter**?   (E ÷ C) + (B – A) = ...

(6)   A = 29   B = 3   C = 19   D = 15   E = 4

What is the answer to this sum **written as a letter**?   (D × B) – (C – B) = ...

(7)   A = 5   B = 16   C = 3   D = 4   E = 8

What is the answer to this sum **written as a letter**?   (A + B) ÷ (D + C) = ...

(8)   A = 9   B = 8   C = 5   D = 4   E = 7

What is the answer to this sum **written as a letter**?   (E × E) – (B × C) = ...

(9)   A = 7   B = 14   C = 19   D = 8   E = 20

What is the answer to this sum **written as a letter**?   (B + C + D) – (B + E) = ...

(10)   A = 4   B = 14   C = 27   D = 3   E = 20

What is the answer to this sum **written as a letter**?   (C ÷ D) + (E ÷ A) = ...

Score: .... / 10

Number Sequences

You have 6 minutes to complete this test.

You have 10 questions to complete within the time given.

For each question, write in the number that completes the sequence.

EXAMPLE

| 34 | 36 | 38 | 40 | 42 | **44** | (The sequence is +2) |

---

(1) 13 4 26 5 52 ....

(2) 9 16 25 36 49 ....

(3) 162 34 142 54 122 ....

(4) 1 4 9 16 25 ....

(5) 37 35 31 25 17 ....

(6) 90 75 60 45 30 ....

(7) 4 12 36 108 324 ....

(8) 2 2 3 5 8 ....

(9) 127 79 55 43 37 ....

(10) 36 20 12 8 6 ....

Score: .... / 10

Word Construction

You have 6 minutes to complete this test.

You have 10 questions to complete within the time given.

In each question, the three words on the second line should go together in the same way as the three words on the first line.

Write in the missing word on the second line.

EXAMPLE

(tame   [meat]   melt)

(bird   [............**rain**............]   yawn)

(word one letter 3, word two letter 2, word one letter 2, word two letter 4)

---

1   (stem   [team]   seat)

     (acne   [....................]   cast)

6   (rags   [ring]   main)

     (line   [....................]   plea)

2   (mile   [lime]   mash)

     (hide   [....................]   coat)

7   (fear   [fret]   sent)

     (pair   [....................]   told)

3   (aunt   [team]   meal)

     (stem   [....................]   told)

8   (wind   [dine]   care)

     (fins   [....................]   rank)

4   (robe   [ruby]   bury)

     (fear   [....................]   glen)

9   (post   [shop]   shoe)

     (echo   [....................]   fold)

5   (show   [hero]   zero)

     (sped   [....................]   core)

10   (king   [skin]   sink)

     (late   [....................]   home)

Score: .... / 10

Double Meanings

In each question, there are two pairs of words. Write in a new word that goes equally well with both word pairs.

EXAMPLE

(item   thing)

(oppose   complain) ....**object**.......

1. (hobby   activity)

   (attract   intrigue) ....

2. (occupied   busy)

   (promised   pledged) ....

3. (story   tale)

   (new   unique) ....

4. (impartial   unbiased)

   (fine   clear) ....

5. (average   mid-point)

   (nasty   unkind) ....

6. (enclosure   cage)

   (ballpoint   felt-tip) ....

7. (volume   work)

   (reserve   schedule) ....

8. (type   sort)

   (caring   gentle) ....

9. (falsehood   fib)

   (recline   rest) ....

10. (pair   unite)

    (game   contest) ....

Score: .... / 10

23

Related Numbers

You have 6 minutes to complete this test.

You have 10 questions to complete within the time given.

In each question, the three numbers in each group are related in some way.

Write in the number that correctly completes the last group.

EXAMPLE

(24   [4]   28)   (21   [2]   23)   (19   [__5__]   24)

(the middle number is the difference between the outer two numbers, i.e. third number minus first number)

① (7   [30]   3)   (8   [41]   4)   (9   [..........]   5)

② (11   [5]   1)   (10   [7]   6)   (16   [..........]   2)

③ (3   [6]   36)   (5   [2]   20)   (11   [..........]   22)

④ (35   [22]   9)   (17   [13]   9)   (31   [..........]   47)

⑤ (4   [12]   8)   (11   [24]   19)   (15   [..........]   34)

⑥ (5   [31]   6)   (6   [48]   12)   (9   [..........]   24)

⑦ (64   [10]   8)   (108   [14]   9)   (84   [..........]   12)

⑧ (13   [28]   5)   (15   [30]   5)   (24   [..........]   6)

⑨ (2   [13]   5)   (4   [71]   7)   (3   [..........]   13)

⑩ (18   [2]   4)   (54   [5]   7)   (99   [..........]   8)

Score: .... / 10

24

You have 6 minutes to complete this test.

You have 10 questions to complete within the time given.

In each question, there are two words in capitals where the letters have been jumbled up.

Rearrange the letters and write the letter that has been removed from both.

EXAMPLE

I brushed my **HTET** before I **WTN** to bed. ....E...............

(*I brushed my TEETH before I WENT to bed.*)

(1) My uncle took me and my **STRSE** to the **FRA** today. ....

(2) Ben likes **TCWHIAG** and **PGLAYI** football at the weekend. ....

(3) The brave **KTNIH** fought the **DRNAO** to the death. ....

(4) Kat likes solving **ARAMNAG** and other **ZPUZLE**. ....

(5) I'm reading a **NVEO** about a shipwrecked **ORSAI**. ....

(6) Yves lost his **EN** silver **CHAT** in the park yesterday. ....

(7) I've forgotten to **DAN** in my **OMERKWO** again! ....

(8) Henry **IPPDSL** and fell on the **CI**. ....

(9) The walkers **IBCLED** to the **MITSU** then rested. ....

(10) We have finally **UBOHG** an **ERICLEC** car. ....

Score: .... / 10

In each question, underline the two words (one from each group) that are most similar in meaning.

EXAMPLE

(<u>champion</u>   plaque   loser)

(leader   trophy   <u>winner</u>)

① (time   minute   first)
(miniscule   hour   second)

⑥ (list   tip   pour)
(sharp   gratuity   straight)

② (anguish   loiter   prefer)
(defraud   fret   encourage)

⑦ (encouraging   opinionated   persuasive)
(convincing   protective   ineffective)

③ (huge   solid   grounded)
(soiled   heavy   realistic)

⑧ (rouse   sleep   engage)
(calm   extricate   excite)

④ (preamble   prim   pristine)
(prudish   shabby   procedure)

⑨ (abundance   permission   altercation)
(argument   agreement   truce)

⑤ (cunning   ignorant   wary)
(crafty   arrogant   honest)

⑩ (mortgage   house   repair)
(building   accommodate   rent)

Score: .... / 10

Antonyms

In each question, underline the two words (one from each group) that are most opposite in meaning.

EXAMPLE

(<u>plentiful</u>   mediocre   intermittent)

(ample   <u>scarce</u>   some)

① (fulfil   restrain   restore)

(reinstate   abolish   pack)

② (severe   solitary   shrill)

(lenient   fair   strict)

③ (pungent   notorious   melancholic)

(prosperous   pessimistic   optimistic)

④ (prominent   unstable   motivated)

(noticeable   inconspicuous   wild)

⑤ (humble   inappropriate   impulsive)

(modest   superior   exhausting)

⑥ (insufferable   indignant   industrious)

(unbearable   appealing   indiscreet)

⑦ (ineffective   mobile   giddy)

(tactless   steady   impulsive)

⑧ (elusive   fragile   dynamic)

(energetic   sluggish   flippant)

⑨ (cordial   honest   contrite)

(trusting   unfriendly   affable)

⑩ (conscientious   bashful   clandestine)

(concealed   obvious   cantankerous)

Score: .... / 10

Word Combinations

You have 6 minutes to complete this test.

You have 10 questions to complete within the time given.

In each question, combine one word from the first group with one word from the second group to create one new word.

The word from the first group always comes first.

Underline the correct word from each group and write in the new word.

EXAMPLE

(clock <u>card</u> car)

(<u>board</u> hand ring)   .... **cardboard** ....

---

(1) (hope   light   penny)

(full   less   more)   ....

(6) (pole   spare   head)

(line   corner   post)   ....

(2) (head   tree   lift)

(top   trick   cap)   ....

(7) (put   set   up)

(about   back   across)   ....

(3) (under   inter   sub)

(mix   start   merge)   ....

(8) (up   over   with)

(stand   place   down)   ....

(4) (tennis   turn   twist)

(table   top   tank)   ....

(9) (gate   bar   lock)

(fence   post   turn)   ....

(5) (foot   hand   hang)

(shoe   shake   glove)   ....

(10) (key   ring   car)

(turn   board   lock)   ....

Score: .... / 10

Complete the Third Pair the Same Way

You have 6 minutes to complete this test.

You have 10 questions to complete within the time given.

Find the word that completes the third pair of words so that it follows the same pattern as the first two pairs.

EXAMPLE

teams seam   fails sail   lands ...._sand_........

(Replace the first letter with the last letter.)

(1) plain pain   spoil soil   cramp ....

(2) breath beat   plant pant   claps ....

(3) case dare   base care   vase ....

(4) patch chat   barge gear   paste ....

(5) barred bead   pamper pear   carrot ....

(6) panther tan   hinder din   centre ....

(7) brave cave   frame game   knock ....

(8) collar oar   slayed led   appear ....

(9) regime mere   arrest star   online ....

(10) lane land   bone bond   mine ....

Score: .... / 10

Missing Three-letter Words

You have 6 minutes to complete this test.

You have 10 questions to complete within the time given.

In each question, three letters have been removed from the word in capitals.

These three letters correctly spell a new word without changing their order.

Write in the three missing letters.

EXAMPLE

Pilar is **PING** carrots for our vegetable soup. .... EEL ....

(*The word in capitals is PEELING.*)

(1) Grandad's many **AILTS** have worsened over the cold winter. ....

(2) Eva bought a fizzy drink from the **VING** machine. ....

(3) Will's **REION** when they won the final was priceless. ....

(4) The teacher asked us to **RERCH** Henry VIII and his wives. ....

(5) The hot and **SWY** marathon runners cooled down with a drink. ....

(6) Cal, a great singer, is now a member of his local **OPTIC** society. ....

(7) **THAND** is a country in Southeast Asia. ....

(8) Sylvie contacted customer **SERVS** to ask about her lost hat. ....

(9) I've packed plenty of warm **CHES** for our weekend away. ....

(10) The teacher **FRED** when we started talking in the test. ....

Score: .... / 10

Code Pairs

Use the alphabet below to help you with these questions.

A B C D E F G H I J K L M N O P Q R S T U V W X Y Z

In each question, use the code provided to identify the new word or code.

EXAMPLE

If the code for **BELT** is **DGNV**, what is the code for **MOST**?   OQUV

(each letter is +2)

---

(1) If the code for **SCARF** is **QXSGR**, what is the code for **GLOVE**?   ....

(2) If the code for **JACKET** is **OMAIOO**, what is **OGKNOM** the code for?   ....

(3) If the code for **THIRST** is **ZYXWVU**, what is the code for **HUNGER**?   ....

(4) If the code for **STOP** is **NWEV**, what is the code for **HALT**?   ....

(5) If the code for **GNOME** is **MHUGK**, what is **NITYE** the code for?   ....

(6) If the code for **WORN** is **DLLM**, what is **IBUL** the code for?   ....

(7) If the code for **SCIENCE** is **TDJFODF**, what is **FOHMJTI** the code for?   ....

(8) If the code for **TREAT** is **ZIUDZ**, what is the code for **SWEET**?   ....

(9) If the code for **STOUT** is **VQRRW**, what is the code for **CLAIM**?   ....

(10) If the code for **PRESSURE** is **KIZJNLMV**, what is the code for **PERSUADE**?   ....

Score: .... / 10

31

Code Sets

You have 6 minutes to complete this test.

You have 9 questions to complete within the time given (3 sets of codes with 3 questions each).

In each set of questions, three of the four words are given in code. These codes are not in the same order as the words and one code is missing. Use these codes to answer each question and write your answer on the dotted line.

EXAMPLE

TALE	LEAP	PEAT	HELP
1532	6251	4236	

Find the code for the word **HELP**.   4236

FOIL	FOWL	GOLF	WOLF
3241	1234	5241	

1. Find the code for the word **WOLF**. ....

2. Find the code for the word **GOLF**. ....

3. Find the word that has the number code **1224**. ....

BAIT	DART	RAID	BIRD
6423	3465	1425	

4. Find the code for the word **RAID**. ....

5. Find the code for the word **BIRD**. ....

6. Find the word that has the number code **3265**. ....

POUR	ROOT	PURE	PORE
5221	3256	3456	

7. Find the code for the word **PURE**. ....

8. Find the code for the word **POUR**. ....

9. Find the word that has the number code **3256**. ....

Score: .... / 9

<table>
<tr><td rowspan="2">**Test**
29</td><td>

Code Sequences

</td></tr>
<tr><td>

You have 6 minutes to complete this test.

You have 10 questions to complete within the time given.

</td></tr>
</table>

Use the alphabet below to help you with these questions.

A B C D E F G H I J K L M N O P Q R S T U V W X Y Z

In each question, find the letters that are next in the sequence.

EXAMPLE

| SL | RM | RN | QO | QP | ......**PQ**...... |

(1st letter −1, 0, −1, 0, −1; 2nd letter +1)

①	MN	LO	KP	JQ	IR	....
②	CH	EF	FE	FE	EF	....
③	VZ	QB	NC	IC	FB	....
④	JJ	OI	MG	QD	PZ	....
⑤	KC	NY	PU	QQ	QM	....
⑥	LS	EZ	XG	QN	JU	....
⑦	KQ	MO	KQ	LP	KQ	....
⑧	BH	AL	DP	CT	FX	....
⑨	AX	BZ	DC	GG	KL	....
⑩	JL	KK	KI	JF	HB	....

Score: .... / 10

Related Words

You have 6 minutes to complete this test.

You have 10 questions to complete within the time given.

In each question, three of the words are related in some way.

Underline the two words that do not relate to the other three.

EXAMPLE

furious   <u>upset</u>   cross   <u>worried</u>   angry

(The underlined words are not synonyms for angry.)

1. barren   dessert   arid   sandy   dry

2. cow   mouse   frog   squirrel   turtle

3. why   who   what   which   that

4. smooth   rough   even   rugged   uneven

5. comma   command   statement   full-stop   exclamation

6. tickets   volume   magazine   book   noise

7. peace   scrap   fragment   material   bit

8. seize   conceal   confiscate   release   impound

9. precious   prudent   sensible   careful   wholesome

10. definite   tentative   consolidated   provisional   unconfirmed

Score: .... / 10

Complete the Sum

You have 6 minutes to complete this test.

You have 10 questions to complete within the time given.

In each question, write in the number that correctly completes the sum.

EXAMPLE

5 + 7 = 3 + ___9___

(1) (9 × 7) − 7 = ... × 8

(2) 72 ÷ 9 + 15 = 11 × 8 − ....

(3) 7^2 − 15 + (6 × 9) = 176 ÷ ....

(4) (17 × 3) − 5 = ... − 17

(5) (63 ÷ 9) + 5 = ... ÷ 9

(6) (15 × 3) − 17 = ... + 3^3

(7) 19 + 18 − (4 × 9) = 1 ÷ ....

(8) 52 − 16 + (6 × 8) = (8 × ....) + 20

(9) (4 × 8) − 10 + 6 = ... − 40

(10) 9 ÷ 3 × 10 + 5 = 7 × ....

Score: .... / 10

Word Analogies

You have 6 minutes to complete this test.

You have 10 questions to complete within the time given.

In each question, underline the two words (one from each group) that will complete the phrase in the best way.

EXAMPLE

Bird is to

(egg <u>fly</u> beak)

as **snake** is to

(poison <u>slither</u> scales)   *(the words are to do with the movement of the animals)*

① **Fling** is to
(cast catch copy)
as **seize** is to
(fall grab hold).

② **America** is to
(Canadian English Armenian)
as **The Netherlands** is to
(Dutch Holland German).

③ **Mobile** is to
(active caravan toy)
as **crude** is to
(arrogant rough oily).

④ **Dog** is to
(domestic canine bark)
as **cheetah** is to
(aggressive safari wild).

⑤ **Succeed** is to
(gain triumph assume)
as **fail** is to
(grasp founder win).

⑥ **Tailor** is to
(cotton tape cloth)
as **carpenter** is to
(pine saw wood).

⑦ **Beacon** is to
(signal hat trace)
as **granule** is to
(fragment corn lump).

⑧ **Chain** is to
(link necklace bike)
as **ladder** is to
(climb window rung).

⑨ **Ornate** is to
(ornament decorative ordinary)
as **shabby** is to
(ruff light scruffy).

⑩ **Botany** is to
(weather plants nature)
as **astronomy** is to
(planets sky observatory).

Score: .... / 10

Letter Connections

In each question, write in the letter that fits into both sets of brackets.

The letter should finish the word before the brackets and start the word after the brackets.

EXAMPLE

ti [......n......] est

te [......n......] ote   (*The four words are tin, nest, ten and note.*)

---

(1) flas [............] erb

whis [............] ite

(2) bre [............] agon

so [............] ard

(3) threa [............] are

chor [............] eny

(4) hal [............] ven

pati [............] ath

(5) wiel [............] onate

bawle [............] unk

(6) gi [............] roan

run [............] ull

(7) trac [............] ink

lin [............] in

(8) cal [............] ode

glu [............] ould

(9) gru [............] east

ver [............] unk

(10) grue [............] ather

trowe [............] inger

Score: .... / 10

Hidden Words

In each question, a four-letter word can be found by combining the end (or whole) of one word with the beginning (or whole) of the next word.

Underline the two words that contain these letters and write in the new four-letter word.

EXAMPLE

We left our bags beside the front door. ....**tour**............. (le**ft our**)

(**1**) Harry said he knew all about the surprise. ....

(**2**) Mum is hoping to buy a brand-new car. ....

(**3**) My sister and I had to watch our baby brother. ....

(**4**) Pietro looked ashamed when he was caught cheating. ....

(**5**) Ursula was angry because she'd missed the bus. ....

(**6**) I didn't flinch at the sight of the huge creature. ....

(**7**) The painter pours ink carefully into the jar. ....

(**8**) The rain meant the picnic was ruined. ....

(**9**) "Don't rush along the corridors," said the teacher. ....

(**10**) There are lots of stars visible tonight. ....

Score: .... / 10

Problem Solving

You have 8 minutes to complete this test.

You have 8 questions to complete within the time given.

In each question, read the information provided and then write in your answer.

EXAMPLE

Alf weighs 19 kg more than Callum.

Callum is twice the weight of Ben, who weighs 12 kg.

How much does Alf weigh?   43 kg

---

(1) Gabriel, Tilly, Jess and Chang attend a gymnastics class after school.
Jess and Chang can do somersaults.
Gabriel and Chang can do handstands.
Everyone apart from Tilly can do backflips.
Everyone apart from Gabriel can do cartwheels and trampoline over the horse.

Who can do the most gymnastic moves?   ....

(2) Eldon thinks of two prime numbers.
He adds the two numbers together.
His answer is 36.

Write all the possible pairs of prime numbers Eldon could be thinking of.   ....

(3) In a marathon, James runs past the person who is in second place.

Which position is James now in?   ....

(4) A 3-metre rope ladder hangs over the side of a boat.
The bottom rung lies on the surface of the water.
The rungs are 15 cm apart, and the tide goes up at a rate of 15 cm per hour.

How long will it be until three rungs are covered?   ....

Questions continue on next page

(5) The temperature in Belfast is the same as Glasgow.

London is 7 degrees warmer than Glasgow but 6 degrees colder than Paris.

Paris is 15 degrees. Taunton is 3 degrees warmer than London.

What is the temperature in Taunton? ....

(6) The post office is west of the school.

Hal's house is south of the school.

The cinema is to the east of the church, and Hal's house is to the north of the church.

What is the direction of the cinema in relation to Hal's house? ....

(7) I start watching a TV programme at 7.10 pm.

The programme is 25 minutes long. After 15 minutes, I pause the programme for ten minutes to make myself a drink and a snack.

At what time do I finish watching my programme? ....

(8) Abdul, Cian, Gina, Freddie and Gaynor are in charge of the football club annual party. They make a list of the food they need: sandwiches, crisps, fruit and pizza.

Cian brings only sandwiches.

Freddie and Gaynor only bring fruit and pizza.

The only thing that Abdul doesn't bring is pizza.

Gina only brings crisps.

How many children do NOT bring sandwiches? ....

Score: .... / 8

Letter Analogies

Use the alphabet below to help you with these questions.

A B C D E F G H I J K L M N O P Q R S T U V W X Y Z

In each question, write in the letters that will complete the phrase in the best way.

EXAMPLE

FG is to **HI** as **ST** is to .... UV ....

(1st letter +2, 2nd letter +2)

---

① **FI** is to **MQ** as **VX** is to ....

② **LK** is to **OP** as **GE** is to ....

③ **MM** is to **KO** as **TT** is to ....

④ **XT** is to **CG** as **RW** is to ....

⑤ **LA** is to **KF** as **SV** is to ....

⑥ **AB** is to **CD** as **WX** is to ....

⑦ **AL** is to **LO** as **CU** is to ....

⑧ **LQ** is to **GV** as **NN** is to ....

⑨ **KI** is to **GH** as **VW** is to ....

⑩ **EB** is to **HE** as **PZ** is to ....

Score: .... / 10

Letters for Numbers

You have **6 minutes** to complete this test.

You have **10 questions** to complete within the time given.

In each question, numbers are shown as letters. Find the answer to the sum and write it in as a letter.

EXAMPLE

A = 2   B = 6   C = 10   D = 5   E = 11
What is the answer to this sum **written as a letter**?   C – D + B = ...**E**....   *(10 – 5 + 6 = 11)*

---

① A = 2   B = 30   C = 3   D = 15   E = 18
What is the answer to this sum **written as a letter**?   (E ÷ C) × A + E = ...

② A = 10   B = 4   C = 12   D = 8   E = 6
What is the answer to this sum **written as a letter**?   B × C ÷ D = ...

③ A = 28   B = 15   C = 17   D = 20   E = 32
What is the answer to this sum **written as a letter**?   B + C + D – D = ...

④ A = 10   B = 6   C = 15   D = 11   E = 22
What is the answer to this sum **written as a letter**?   (C – A) × E ÷ A = ...

⑤ A = 20   B = 24   C = 6   D = 4   E = 40
What is the answer to this sum **written as a letter**?   (B ÷ C) + (E – B) = ...

⑥ A = 9   B = 6   C = 11   D = 27   E = 30
What is the answer to this sum **written as a letter**?   (B × C) – (A + D) = ...

⑦ A = 15   B = 2   C = 11   D = 14   E = 28
What is the answer to this sum **written as a letter**?   (E ÷ D) + (B + C) = ...

⑧ A = 19   B = 8   C = 6   D = 4   E = 7
What is the answer to this sum **written as a letter**?   (B × E) – (B × C) = ...

⑨ A = 1   B = 14   C = 12   D = 4   E = 36
What is the answer to this sum **written as a letter**?   (E ÷ C) + (B – C – A) = ...

⑩ A = 4   B = 14   C = 27   D = 3   E = 20
What is the answer to this sum **written as a letter**?   (C ÷ D) + (E ÷ A) = ...

Score: .... / 10

For each question, write in the number that completes the sequence.

EXAMPLE

34   36   38   40   42   ....**44**........   *(The sequence is +2)*

①   144   121   100   81   64   ....

②   2   5   4   7   6   ....

③   −16   −11   −6   −1   4   ....

④   67   68   70   73   77   ....

⑤   1   1   2   3   5   ....

⑥   88   73   60   49   40   ....

⑦   7   50   8   65   9   ....

⑧   81   72   64   57   51   ....

⑨   108   96   84   72   60   ....

⑩   2   5   9   14   20   ....

Score: .... / 10

Word Construction

You have 6 minutes to complete this test.

You have 10 questions to complete within the time given.

In each question, the three words on the second line should go together in the same way as the three words on the first line.

Write in the missing word on the second line.

EXAMPLE

(tame   [meat]   melt)

(bird   [...... *rain* ......]   yawn)

(word one letter 3, word two letter 2, word one letter 2, word two letter 4)

1) (pear   [rank]   mink)

   (rain   [.....................]   lace)

2) (bath   [bash]   bins)

   (hale   [.....................]   deck)

3) (post   [stop]   coup)

   (pore   [.....................]   send)

4) (else   [sell]   alas)

   (unit   [.....................]   part)

5) (ache   [heal]   also)

   (bite   [.....................]   stop)

6) (sane   [ease]   each)

   (mine   [.....................]   tyre)

7) (sham   [most]   told)

   (alas   [.....................]   meal)

8) (rake   [beak]   able)

   (crew   [.....................]   area)

9) (save   [ever]   rent)

   (pert   [.....................]   pill)

10) (pale   [reap]   star)

   (polo   [.....................]   hash)

Score: .... / 10

Double Meanings

You have 6 minutes to complete this test.

You have 10 questions to complete within the time given.

In each question, there are two pairs of words. Write in a new word that goes equally well with both word pairs.

EXAMPLE

(item   thing)

(oppose   complain) ....**object**............

---

(1) (stem   shoot)

    (follow   pursue)   ....

(2) (waterhole   spring)

    (healthy   fit)   ....

(3) (topic   theme)

    (happy   satisfied)   ....

(4) (company   business)

    (hard   solid)   ....

(5) (basin   dish)

    (throw   launch)   ....

(6) (tire   exhaust)

    (drill   mine)   ....

(7) (degree   size)

    (mount   ascend)   ....

(8) (horizontal   even)

    (destroy   wreck)   ....

(9) (sketch   design)

    (pull   drag)   ....

(10) (illuminate   brighten)

    (pale   fair)   ....

Score: .... / 10

Related Numbers

You have 6 minutes to complete this test.

You have 10 questions to complete within the time given.

In each question, the three numbers in each group are related in some way.

Write in the number that correctly completes the last group.

EXAMPLE

(24   [4]   28)   (21   [2]   23)   (19   [__5__]   24)

(the middle number is the difference between the outer two numbers, i.e. third number minus first number)

①   (10   [4]   39)   (7   [8]   55)   (12   [..............]   143)

②   (19   [24]   25)   (37   [32]   45)   (57   [..............]   69)

③   (3^2 [5] 2^2)   (5^2 [9] 4^2)   (11^2 [..............] 8^2)

④   (75   [14]   5)   (78   [25]   3)   (96   [..............]   4)

⑤   (112   [16]   14)   (96   [8]   24)   (78   [..............]   26)

⑥   (2^2 [14] 3^2)   (4^2 [42] 5^2)   (6^2 [..............] 7^2)

⑦   (17   [72]   19)   (23   [104]   29)   (57   [..............]   39)

⑧   (78   [27]   24)   (97   [19]   59)   (89   [..............]   37)

⑨   (13   [117]   3)   (15   [135]   3)   (17   [..............]   3)

⑩   (66   [9]   11)   (56   [10]   8)   (42   [..............]   6)

Score: .... / 10

Jumbled Words with a Letter Removed

In each question, there are two words in capitals where the letters have been jumbled up.

Rearrange the letters and write the letter that has been removed from both.

EXAMPLE

I brushed my **HTET** before I **WTN** to bed. ....E................

(I brushed my TEETH before I WENT to bed.)

1. Ursula had rice **SAKE** with a glass of **UJIE**. ....

2. The horse **LEL** at the **STIR** hurdle. ....

3. Dad placed **LAC** and **LSG** on the fire. ....

4. The **LITUAY** of the food was **TUIE** poor. ....

5. Maeve likes **CLEDRSMB** egg with **STOT**. ....

6. I've been **GREISIN** for my **DINGRI** test all day. ....

7. Tom is **IGTRAELVL RAODU** the Greek islands. ....

8. The **BAEYTT** on my phone keeps losing its **AGCHE**. ....

9. Mum is **CGTIUN** the grass before it **RATSS** raining. ....

10. Jen's new puppy is really **TUE** and **DUDYL**. ....

Score: .... / 10

Synonyms

In each question, underline the two words (one from each group) that are most similar in meaning.

EXAMPLE

(champion   plaque   loser)

(leader   trophy   winner)

---

1 (nominee   head   choice)

(resignation   candidate   deputy)

2 (deposit   bank   recede)

(profit   withdraw   proceed)

3 (respectful   loyal   honorary)

(dismissive   majestic   faithful)

4 (misinform   misinterpret   misunderstand)

(mislead   misfortune   misalign)

5 (weather   howl   meander)

(hail   wind   rain)

6 (barge   canal   river)

(float   push   sail)

7 (seeds   cultivate   root)

(grow   disperse   earth)

8 (apply   appear   adhere)

(stick   contact   admonish)

9 (cache   bank   count)

(store   money   coins)

10 (weird   askew   grumpy)

(aligned   awry   level)

Score: .... / 10

Antonyms

In each question, underline the two words (one from each group) that are most opposite in meaning.

EXAMPLE

(<u>plentiful</u>   mediocre   intermittent)

(ample   <u>scarce</u>   some)

① (appease   avert   avoid)

(pacify   provoke   attract)

② (competent   benign   copious)

(abundant   able   scarce)

③ (fly   exploit   escalate)

(destroy   promote   diminish)

④ (prosperous   tireless   pungent)

(wealthy   relentless   idle)

⑤ (proficient   optimistic   motivated)

(skilled   blatant   incompetent)

⑥ (trivial   valiant   insidious)

(frivolous   negligible   important)

⑦ (stealthy   taut   squeamish)

(delicate   tough   shrill)

⑧ (final   painstaking   resilient)

(careless   recovered   well)

⑨ (reticent   solitary   feeble)

(uncommunicative   frank   efficient)

⑩ (tentative   vile   viscous)

(thick   thorough   watery)

Score: .... / 10

Word Combinations

In each question, combine one word from the first group with one word from the second group to create one new word.

The word from the first group always comes first.

Underline the correct word from each group and write in the new word.

EXAMPLE

(clock   card   car)

(board   hand   ring)   _cardboard_

---

① (scare   bird   score)

(point   count   crow)   ....

② (shell   sea   fresh)

(food   air   breeze)   ....

③ (after   before   miss)

(think   thinking   thought)   ....

④ (up   walk   show)

(behind   down   with)   ....

⑤ (gold   silver   bronze)

(weir   wear   ware)   ....

⑥ (broad   narrow   for)

(cast   iron   metal)   ....

⑦ (follow   trail   lead)

(blazer   after   track)   ....

⑧ (before   right   with)

(stock   place   hand)   ....

⑨ (rich   life   fashion)

(style   model   wealth)   ....

⑩ (shelf   frame   free)

(ledge   dome   lance)   ....

Score: .... / 10

Complete the Third Pair the Same Way

Find the word that completes the third pair of words so that it follows the same pattern as the first two pairs.

EXAMPLE

teams seam   fails sail   lands ....**sand**............

(Replace the first letter with the last letter.)

(1) keeper reek   editor rode   rather ....

(2) follow wolf   skills skis   pastor ....

(3) message age   stopping pit   wanders ....

(4) space spade   cars cart   slice ....

(5) mechanic name   chapter etch   student ....

(6) sidle lid   table lab   bugle ....

(7) waist waste   aisle isle   bridle ....

(8) stump pump   treat teat   clash ....

(9) crispy sip   sooty toy   plaster ....

(10) tread trod   go went   read ....

Score: .... / 10

Missing Three-letter Words

You have 6 minutes to complete this test.

You have 10 questions to complete within the time given.

In each question, three letters have been removed from the word in capitals.

These three letters correctly spell a new word without changing their order.

Write in the three missing letters.

EXAMPLE

Pilar is **PING** carrots for our vegetable soup. ....EEL...........

(The word in capitals is PEELING.)

1. The king's **SERTS** brought him a golden goblet of wine. ....

2. Due to lack of **ANCES**, the new building has been put on hold. ....

3. The fire-breathing **DON** guarded the cave with his life. ....

4. Harry used home-made **PAS** for his apple pie. ....

5. Our new neighbours greeted us **WLY** when we moved in. ....

6. In the **BL** of an eye, my baby sister has turned four! ....

7. Toni worked through the calculation on the **BD**. ....

8. My talented brother is a **DING** classical pianist. ....

9. My new novel's **TE** is the gap between the rich and the poor. ....

10. Ged's garden is renowned for its bright **COLS** in the spring. ....

Score: .... / 10

Code Pairs

Use the alphabet below to help you with these questions.

A B C D E F G H I J K L M N O P Q R S T U V W X Y Z

In each question, use the code provided to identify the new word or code.

EXAMPLE

If the code for **BELT** is **DGNV**, what is the code for **MOST**?   OQUV

(each letter is +2)

1. If the code for **LIGHT** is **ILDKQ**, what is the code for **WEIGH**? ....

2. If the code for **HEAVY** is **IFBWZ**, what is **TNBMM** the code for? ....

3. If the code for **TALENT** is **VYOBQP**, what is the code for **GIFTED**? ....

4. If the code for **MOTHER** is **IWTPAJ**, what is **BITPAJ** the code for? ....

5. If the code for **WINDY** is **DRMWB**, what is the code for **RAINY**? ....

6. If the code for **ATTEND** is **ZRQAIX**, what is the code for **IGNORE**? ....

7. If the code for **SULKY** is **HLEFV**, what is **HDBGB** the code for? ....

8. If the code for **HORSE** is **JNUQI**, what is the code for **ZEBRA**? ....

9. If the code for **GRAPE** is **FEDCB**, what is the code for **WINES**? ....

10. If the code for **GIVE** is **HJWF**, what word is **UBLF** the code for? ....

Score: .... / 10

Code Sets

You have 6 minutes to complete this test.

You have 9 questions to complete within the time given
(3 sets of codes with 3 questions each).

In each set of questions, three of the four words are given in code. These codes are not in the same order as the words and one code is missing. Use these codes to answer each question and write your answer on the dotted line.

EXAMPLE

TALE	LEAP	PEAT	HELP
1532	6251	4236	

Find the code for the word **HELP**.   4236

SEAT	LAST	STEM	MEAL
6325	5241	4321	

(1) Find the code for the word **MEAL**.   ....

(2) Find the code for the word **MATE**.   ....

(3) Find the word that has the number code **4326**.   ....

NEED	DARN	REAR	RARE
1234	3235	4551	

(4) Find the code for the word **DARN**.   ....

(5) Find the code for the word **REAR**.   ....

(6) Find the word that has the number code **4523**.   ....

LANE	LEAN	PALE	TAPE
6351	4132	4321	

(7) Find the code for the word **PALE**.   ....

(8) Find the code for the word **TAPE**.   ....

(9) Find the word that has the number code **2351**.   ....

Score: .... / 9

Code Sequences

You have 6 minutes to complete this test.

You have 10 questions to complete within the time given.

Use the alphabet below to help you with these questions.

A B C D E F G H I J K L M N O P Q R S T U V W X Y Z

In each question, find the letters that are next in the sequence.

EXAMPLE

SL	RM	RN	QO	QP	<u>PQ</u>

(1st letter –1, 0, –1, 0, –1; 2nd letter +1)

---

1.   OP   RM   PO   SL   QN   ....

2.   DL   GJ   CI   FI   BJ   ....

3.   DD   EB   GA   HY   JX   ....

4.   PK   UA   ZQ   EG   JW   ....

5.   JY   LW   PS   VM   DE   ....

6.   LN   ES   XX   QC   JH   ....

7.   KQ   NO   MP   ON   MP   ....

8.   BH   XL   DP   HT   BX   ....

9.   AB   BA   DY   GV   KR   ....

10.   QY   MV   RS   NP   SM   ....

Score: .... / 10

Test	# Related Words
51	You have 6 minutes to complete this test. You have 10 questions to complete within the time given.

In each question, three of the words are related in some way.

Underline the two words that do not relate to the other three.

EXAMPLE

furious   <u>upset</u>   cross   <u>worried</u>   angry

(The underlined words are not synonyms for angry.)

1.   lucid   fashionable   quirky   clear   comprehensible

2.   Asia   Ireland   Africa   France   Antarctica

3.   churlish   giddy   frail   surly   ill-tempered

4.   chest   rib   spine   finger   skull

5.   truck   canoe   ferry   ship   caravan

6.   ram   foal   cygnet   ring   colt

7.   teaspoon   fork   dish   knife   cup

8.   dangerous   suspicious   disabled   unsure   dubious

9.   concur   conflict   strife   clash   agree

10.   box   run   fight   spar   flee

Score: .... / 10

Complete the Sum

In each question, write in the number that correctly completes the sum.

EXAMPLE

$5 + 7 = 3 +$ ......**9**......

(1) $27 \div 3 + 5 - 5 =$ .... $\div 9$

(2) $40 \div 8 + 10 = (2 \times$ ....$) + 9$

(3) $180 - 95 - 62 = 31 -$ ....

(4) $6^2 + 30 = 11 \times$ .... $- 11$

(5) $(12 \times 7) - 5^2 =$ .... $\times 8 + 3$

(6) $18 \div 3 + (8 \times 9) = 9^2 - ($..................... $\times 3)$

(7) $(7 \times 8) + (3 \times 15) = (3 \times 25) +$ ....

(8) $15 + 16 - (3 \times 9) = 56 \div$ ....

(9) $7 + 8 - (9 \times 1) = (7 \times 3) -$ ....

(10) $(3 \times 8) + 16 - 9 =$ .... $+ (4 \times 6)$

Score: .... / 10

Word Analogies

You have 6 minutes to complete this test.

You have 10 questions to complete within the time given.

In each question, underline the two words (one from each group) that will complete the phrase in the best way.

EXAMPLE

Bird is to

(egg <u>fly</u> beak)

as **snake** is to

(poison <u>slither</u> scales)   (*the words are to do with the movement of the animals*)

---

(1) **Violin** is to

(string bow fiddle)

as **joiner** is to

(carpenter attachment wood).

(2) **Paw** is to

(hand thumb beg)

as **snout** is to

(pig nose snuffle).

(3) **Apple** is to

(orchard pips skin)

as **grape** is to

(wine bunch vineyard).

(4) **Find** is to

(lose loose lost)

as **seize** is to

(hold push release).

(5) **Foal** is to

(gelding mare colt)

as **kid** is to

(nanny lamb boar).

(6) **Cake** is to

(flower flour icing)

as **omelette** is to

(eggs fry pan).

(7) **Recover** is to

(healthy rescue armchair)

as **sanction** is to

(punish law disapprove).

(8) **Bold** is to

(font dark cheeky)

as **italics** is to

(highlight underline slant).

(9) **Fox** is to

(badger sly wild)

as **dog** is to

(bark gerbil wolf).

(10) **Hilarious** is to

(dull funny interesting)

as **ludicrous** is to

(shocking hesitant ridiculous).

Score: .... / 10

Letter Connections

You have 6 minutes to complete this test.

You have 10 questions to complete within the time given.

In each question, write in the letter that fits into both sets of brackets.

The letter should finish the word before the brackets and start the word after the brackets.

EXAMPLE

ti [....n....] est

te [....n....] ote   (*The four words are tin, nest, ten and note.*)

---

1 lam [..............] enign

com [..............] olt

2 gra [..............] aid

cal [..............] ute

3 woo [..............] end

bel [..............] oot

4 wrat [..............] ind

wis [..............] ail

5 clas [..............] int

fli [..............] ink

6 spe [..............] ew

free [..............] ark

7 mist [..............] earn

hol [..............] elp

8 kee [..............] aval

stu [..............] ine

9 blen [..............] une

mai [..............] eluge

10 pal [..............] ink

groo [..............] ood

Score: .... / 10

Hidden Words

You have 6 minutes to complete this test.

You have 10 questions to complete within the time given.

In each question, a four-letter word can be found by combining the end (or whole) of one word with the beginning (or whole) of the next word.

Underline the two words that contain these letters and write in the new four-letter word.

EXAMPLE

We left our bags beside the front door.   ......**tour**......   (left our)

---

1 A cup of tea makes Mum very happy.   ....

2 "I double dare you!" said Jake to his big brother.   ....

3 Curious, Ushma peered over a cliff edge despite the warnings.   ....

4 A car crash unfortunately delayed my journey to the airport.   ....

5 I'm always more alert after a strong cup of coffee.   ....

6 Sam wished his puppy would stay forever young.   ....

7 Gina said the first book in the series was her favourite.   ....

8 Mum wore her best dress to my birthday meal.   ....

9 Her alarm rang but Grace kept her eyes closed.   ....

10 Ricky wasn't a bit interested in what I had to say.   ....

Score: .... / 10

Problem Solving

In each question, read the information provided and then write in your answer.

EXAMPLE

Alf weighs 19 kg more than Callum.

Callum is twice the weight of Ben, who weighs 12 kg.

How much does Alf weigh?   .... *43 kg* ....

---

(1) Vita, Baz, Carl, Fay and Wenda all like salt and pepper in their soup.

Wenda likes carrots, parsnips and leeks in her soup.

Everyone apart from Fay likes lentils in their soup.

Only Baz and Vita like chilli in theirs, and only Carl likes garlic in his.

Which child likes everything in their soup apart from chilli and garlic?   ....

(2) Luigi and Franco come to school by car.

Eric takes the bus or train.

Isaac rides his bike but sometimes walks.

Mo gets a lift with Franco.

Maya lives far away and takes the train if she misses the bus.

How many children come to school by car?   ....

(3) Finn, Oisìn, Joe, Molly and Becki each make a fruit salad.

Joe and Oisìn only use apples, pears and pineapples, while Molly only uses apples and pineapples.

Becki and Finn use everything except pears and raspberries.

Who uses the least fruit in their fruit salad?   ....

Questions continue on next page

(4) Zac, Florence, Chloe, Marje and Zainab are discussing their favourite subjects.

All the children enjoy art.

Everyone apart from Florence likes PE.

Only Marje and Zac like music.

Zainab enjoys English and history, but not maths.

Florence and Chloe like maths but not English.

Which two subjects are the least popular? .... and ....

(5) Chan, Laurie, Ganesh, Ciara and Elsie are competing in a running race.

The fastest got to the winning post in 6 minutes and 25 seconds.

Ciara finished 2 minutes before Laurie.

Elsie finished 35 seconds after Ganesh.

Chan and Laurie finished at the same time.

Laurie finished in 8 minutes 45 seconds.

Who came third? ....

(6) Five babies are born on the same day.

The smallest baby weighs 2.6 kg.

Baby D weighs 0.2 kg more than Baby B.

Baby A weighs 1 kg more than Baby C.

Baby E weighs the same as Baby B. Baby E weighs 3.4 kg.

How much does Baby A weigh? .... kg

(7) A group of four children in Year 6 discuss the colour of their eyes.

Ralf does not have blue eyes.

Danny does not have green eyes.

Grainne has brown eyes and Danny has hazel eyes.

Sabine's eyes are not blue and not the same colour as Ralf's or Danny's.

Grainne has the same colour eyes as Ralf.

Danny's eyes are not the same colour as Ralf's or Grainne's.

What colour are Sabine's eyes? ....

(8) Abhati is three years younger than Mabel will be next year.

Angus is thirteen.

Mabel is two years older than Angus was last year.

How old is Abhati? ....

Letter Analogies

You have 6 minutes to complete this test.

You have 10 questions to complete within the time given.

Use the alphabet below to help you with these questions.

A B C D E F G H I J K L M N O P Q R S T U V W X Y Z

In each question, write in the letters that will complete the phrase in the best way.

EXAMPLE

FG is to **HI** as **ST** is to ....UV.............

(1st letter +2, 2nd letter +2)

---

1. **HD** is to **LO** as **QT** is to ....

2. **WZ** is to **DA** as **OR** is to ....

3. **XT** is to **QA** as **KN** is to ....

4. **YW** is to **SQ** as **QY** is to ....

5. **RB** is to **ZG** as **TK** is to ....

6. **PQ** is to **LK** as **DE** is to ....

7. **NU** is to **MU** as **JO** is to ....

8. **JH** is to **EK** as **DI** is to ....

9. **LT** is to **RI** as **VU** is to ....

10. **NO** is to **HI** as **GF** is to ....

Score: .... / 10

Letters for Numbers

In each question, numbers are shown as letters. Find the answer to the sum and write it in as a letter.

EXAMPLE

A = 2   B = 6   C = 10   D = 5   E = 11

What is the answer to this sum **written as a letter**?   C − D + B = ___E___   (10 − 5 + 6 = 11)

---

(1) A = 12   B = 16   C = 9   D = 5   E = 25

What is the answer to this sum **written as a letter**?   (B + C + D) − D = ...

(2) A = 8   B = 4   C = 14   D = 19   E = 7

What is the answer to this sum **written as a letter**?   B × C ÷ A = ...

(3) A = 12   B = 20   C = 7   D = 15   E = 28

What is the answer to this sum **written as a letter**?   (E ÷ C) × A − E = ...

(4) A = 20   B = 49   C = 7   D = 25   E = 38

What is the answer to this sum **written as a letter**?   (B ÷ C) + (E − A) = ...

(5) A = 27   B = 4   C = 16   D = 24   E = 13

What is the answer to this sum **written as a letter**?   (B × C) − (D + E) = ...

(6) A = 17   B = 12   C = 23   D = 10   E = 34

What is the answer to this sum **written as a letter**?   (C − A) × (E ÷ A) = ...

(7) A = 132   B = 42   C = 3   D = 14   E = 7

What is the answer to this sum **written as a letter**?   (B ÷ E) + (B × C) = ...

(8) A = 44   B = 12   C = 25   D = 4   E = 28

What is the answer to this sum **written as a letter**?   (E ÷ D) + (B + C) = ...

(9) A = 4   B = 20   C = 42   D = 3   E = 24

What is the answer to this sum **written as a letter**?   (C ÷ D) + (E ÷ A) = ...

(10) A = 8   B = 144   C = 12   D = 28   E = 36

What is the answer to this sum **written as a letter**?   (B ÷ C) + (E − C − A) = ...

Score: .... / 10

Test 59	**Number Sequences**	
	You have 6 minutes to complete this test.	
	You have 10 questions to complete within the time given.	

For each question, write in the number that completes the sequence.

EXAMPLE

34	36	38	40	42	<u>44</u>	*(The sequence is +2)*

1.   7   6   6   7   9   ....

2.   10   13   17   22   28   ....

3.   80   63   48   35   24   ....

4.   84   124   42   62   21   ....

5.   2   3   5   7   11   ....

6.   87   86   83   78   71   ....

7.   1   8   27   64   125   ....

8.   1   1   2   6   24   ....

9.   420   390   360   330   300   ....

10.   −18   17   −14   13   −10   ....

Score: .... / 10

Word Construction

You have 6 minutes to complete this test.

You have 10 questions to complete within the time given.

In each question, the three words on the second line should go together in the same way as the three words on the first line.

Write in the missing word on the second line.

EXAMPLE

(tame   [meat]   melt)

(bird   [......rain......]   yawn)

(word one letter 3, word two letter 2, word one letter 2, word two letter 4)

---

1 (heal   [sale]   cash)

(pelt   [..................]   carp)

2 (dire   [read]   fear)

(rake   [..................]   shed)

3 (pace   [cape]   cope)

(neat   [..................]   date)

4 (same   [mite]   wilt)

(cute   [..................]   corn)

5 (fair   [raft]   tuft)

(hear   [..................]   want)

6 (rush   [bush]   verb)

(sash   [..................]   limb)

7 (dark   [lark]   luck)

(rind   [..................]   sick)

8 (brag   [gain]   bind)

(mean   [..................]   file)

9 (damp   [blip]   limb)

(flog   [..................]   lump)

10 (fear   [fret]   lint)

(pour   [..................]   sold)

Score: .... / 10

Answers

Test 1 Synonyms

Q1 squander, waste

Q2 limit, restrict

Q3 cascade, waterfall

Q4 burgle, steal

Q5 unlawful, illicit

Q6 succumb, surrender

Q7 deflect, divert

Q8 shroud, covering

Q9 phoney, fake

Q10 sparse, scarce

Test 2 Antonyms

Q1 fragile, robust

Q2 indifferent, concerned

Q3 chaotic, controlled

Q4 inhibited, spontaneous

Q5 jubilant, sad

Q6 lavish, meagre

Q7 valiant, cowardly

Q8 virtuous, corrupt

Q9 surplus, deficiency

Q10 scrupulous, slapdash

Test 3 Word Combinations

Q1 foreground (fore and ground)

Q2 floodgates (flood and gates)

Q3 antelope (ant and elope)

Q4 warehouse (ware and house)

Q5 fingertip (finger and tip)

Q6 newsagent (news and agent)

Q7 handsome (hand and some)

Q8 however (how and ever)

Q9 underline (under and line)

Q10 adaptable (adapt and able)

Test 4 Complete the Third Pair the Same Way

Q1 flunk (change the 'a' to a 'u')

Q2 gun (move the first letter one letter along the alphabet)

Q3 nest (last two letters reversed followed by third and fourth letters)

Q4 menu (number code 1634)

Q5 pro (last letter followed by previous two letters)

Q6 rough (one letter in, three-letter word; two letters in, four-letter word; three letters in, five-letter word)

Q7 step (number code 3451)

Q8 sole (number code 1235)

Q9 are (number code 423)

Q10 soil (replace first letter with an 's')

Test 5 Missing Three-letter Words

Q1 SIN (the word in capitals is **BUSINESS**)

Q2 NIT (the word in capitals is **IGNITED**)

Q3 CAP (the word in capitals is **ESCAPED**)

Q4 HER (the word in capitals is **INHERITED**)

Q5 TAN (the word in capitals is **CIRCUMSTANCES**)

Q6 BUN (the word in capitals is **BUNDLE**)

Q7 ARE (the word in capitals is **APPARENT**)

Q8 RAN (the word in capitals is **STRANGE**)

Q9 TEN (the word in capitals is **CONTENTEDLY**)

Q10 RAT (the word in capitals is **CRATERS**)

Test 6 Code Pairs

Q1 VHMF (−1, −1, −1, −1)

Q2 NRPQ (+1, +3, +1, +3)

Q3 HELP (The code for TIPS to UHQR is +1, −1, +1, −1. So, to find the word from IDMO, reverse the code to −1, +1, −1, +1)

Q4 WDWGGBU (+5, −1, +4, −2, +3, −3, +2)

Q5 DUYSGRR (+2, −10, −5, +1, −8, +3, +5)

Test 6 answers continue on next page

Q6 FLOWER (The code for STICKY to QPCUAM is −2, −4, −6, −8, −10, −12. So, to find the word from DHIOUF, reverse the code to +2, +4, +6, +8, +10, +12)

Q7 IRQL (+3, +9, +5, +7)

Q8 WEPXKM (+4, +10, 0, +8, +6, −5)

Q9 KKM (+7, −7, −12)

Q10 CLJSX (−9, +11, −8, +12, −7)

Test 7 Code Sets

Q1 6352

Q2 4352

Q3 MEAL

Q4 3142

Q5 2134

Q6 DEAF

Q7 4365

Q8 6315

Q9 LASH

Test 8 Code Sequences

Q1 HJ (1st letter: +5, +4, +3, +2, +1; 2nd letter: −4, −3, −2, −1, 0)

Q2 ON (1st letter: +3, +4, +3, +4, +3; 2nd letter: −4, −3, −4, −3, −4)

Q3 JU (1st letter: −1, −2, −3, −4, −5; 2nd letter: −2, −1, −2, −1, −2)

Q4 VF (1st letter: +3, +6, +3, +6, +3; 2nd letter: −2)

Q5 AW (1st letter: −1; 2nd letter: +1, +4, +1, +4, +1)

Q6 SK (1st letter: +1; 2nd letter: +2)

Q7 RL (1st letter: −2; 2nd letter: +2)

Q8 VS (1st letter: −5; 2nd letter: −5)

Q9 MJ (1st letter: +2, +4, +6, +8, +10; 2nd letter: −8, −6, −4, −2, 0)

Q10 JS (1st letter: +3, −1, +3, −1, +3; 2nd letter: −3, +1, −3, +1, −3)

Test 9 Related Words

Q1 spoon, pan (all the others are types of crockery)

Q2 horse, bull (all the others are female animals)

Q3 let, permit (all the others are synonyms for choose)

Q4 rich, successful (all the others are synonyms for aspiring)

Q5 apple, grape (all the others are places where fruit or vegetables grow)

Q6 burrow, nest (all the others are human-made animal homes)

Q7 meagre, beautiful (all the others are synonyms for ornate)

Q8 sun, wind (all the others are types of weather that involve water)

Q9 tick, smack (all the others are synonyms for mark and can be found on the skin)

Q10 subject, topic (all the others are synonyms for aim)

Test 10 Complete the Sum

Q1 6

Q2 4

Q3 25

Q4 4

Q5 48

Q6 9

Q7 45

Q8 9

Q9 3

Q10 4

Test 11 Word Analogies

Q1 nose, ear (the words relate to the body parts used for smelling and hearing)

Q2 satisfied, worried (the words are synonyms)

Q3 vehicle, vessel (the words both describe the type of transport)

Q4 odd, smooth (the words are antonyms)

Q5 clash, falter (the words are synonyms)

Q6 key, string (the words are how the sound is produced on each instrument)

Q7 mysterious, brittle (the words are synonyms)

Q8 childhood, railway (the words are compound words)

Q9 lethargic, useless (the words are antonyms)

Q10 determined, beautiful (the words are synonyms)

Test 12 Letter Connections

Q1 r (the four words are far, ripe, car, rent)

Q2 w (the four words are sew, war, paw, wet)

Q3 n (the four words are loin, nag, bun, nil)

Q4 l (the four words are fill, lip, poll, lob)

Q5 p (the four words are grip, pup, pip, pig)

Q6 y (the four words are pay, youth, buoy, yap)

Q7 t (the four words are spent, tame, grant, taint)

Q8 c (the four words are toxic, cable, arc, chafe)

Q9 p (the four words are flip, pony, trap, pledge)

Q10 y (the four words are key, yearn, tray, yawn)

Test 13 Hidden Words

Q1 mean (sa**me an**swer)

Q2 sick (ba**sic k**nowledge)

Q3 vein (ha**ve in**vested)

Q4 fore (**for e**xtra)

Q5 able (**a ble**ating)

Q6 sour (i**s our**)

Q7 them (**the m**agnificent)

Q8 knew (o'cloc**k new**s)

Q9 herd (neit**her d**id)

Q10 tone (a**t one**)

Test 14 Problem Solving

Q1 **Ahmed**

	Seb	Stella	Erin	Joe	Ahmed
bins	✓	✓	✓	✓	✗
washing up		✓	✓	✓	
walk dog		✓			✓
floors	✓	✓	✓	✗	✗
dusting				✓	
feed dog		✓			

Q2 **7.45 pm**

7.55 pm is actually 8.20 pm if the clock is 25 minutes slow. 8.20 pm less 35 minutes is 7.45 pm.

Q3 **Freddy**

If Freddy is Carl's father's father, he must be Carl's grandfather.

Q4 **August 1994**

Guy was born 3 years and 8 months before Fay.

Q5 **Eve**

	Mo	Ethan	Eve
hockey	✓	?	?
choir	✗	✓	✓
football	✓	✗	✓
art	?	?	✓

It's possible that Mo and Ethan are members of 3 clubs, but Eve definitely is.

Q6 **£3136.50**

25% of £12,546 = £3136.50

Q7 **£65**

Klaus	Petra	Chen	Ivy	Ruby
£65 (80 − 15 = 65)	£75	£25 (75 ÷ 3 = 25)	£12.50 (25 ÷ 2 = 12.50)	£80

Ruby must have raised the highest amount at £80, so Klaus raises £65 less than Ruby.

Q8 **25 years old**

Carla	Beth	Max
25 (2.5 × 10 = 25)	10 (15 − 5 = 10)	15 (we are told Max is 15)

Test 15 Letter Analogies

Q1 GN (1st letter +4, 2nd letter −4)

Q2 LK (1st letter −1, 2nd letter −1)

Q3 FU (1st letter +2, 2nd letter −2)

Q4 TP (1st letter −2, 2nd letter −2)

Q5 BA (1st letter +5, 2nd letter +5)

Q6 ZC (1st letter −5, 2nd letter +7)

Q7 GD (1st letter −3, 2nd letter +3)

Q8 RI (1st letter −4, 2nd letter −4)

Q9 SW (1st letter +8, 2nd letter 0)

Q10 HQ (1st letter +1, 2nd letter −3)

Test 16 Letters for Numbers

Q1 E

Q2 B

Q3 D

Q4 B

Test 16 answers continue on next page

Q5 D
Q6 A
Q7 C
Q8 A
Q9 A
Q10 B

Test 17 Number Sequences

Q1 6 (the sequence is every other one doubled and +1)

Q2 64 (the sequence is square numbers)

Q3 74 (the sequence is every other one −20 and +20)

Q4 36 (the sequence is adding consecutive odd numbers +3, +5, +7, +9, +11)

Q5 7 (the sequence is subtracting consecutive even numbers −2, −4, −6, −8, −10)

Q6 15 (the sequence is −15)

Q7 972 (the sequence is ×3)

Q8 12 (the sequence is +0, +1, +2, +3, +4)

Q9 34 (the sequence is −48, −24, −12, −6, −3)

Q10 5 (the sequence is −16, −8, −4, −2, −1)

Test 18 Word Construction

Q1 case (word one letter 2, word two letters 2 and 3, word one letter 4)

Q2 dice (word one letters 3 and 2, word two letter 1, word one letter 4)

Q3 most (word one letter 4, word two letter 2, word one letter 1, word two letter 1)

Q4 flan (word one letter 1, word two letter 2, word one letter 3, word two letter 4)

Q5 pore (word one letter 2, word two letter 2, word two letter 3, word one letter 3 OR word two letter 4)

Q6 lean (word one letter 1, word two letter 3, word two letter 4, word one letter 3)

Q7 prod (word one letter 1, word one letter 4, word two letter 2, word two letter 4)

Q8 sink (word one letter 4, word one letter 2, word one letter 3, word two letter 4)

Q9 hole (word one letter 3, word two letter 2, word two letter 3, word one letter 1)

Q10 heat (word two letter 1, word two letter 4, word one letter 2, word one letter 3)

Test 19 Double Meanings

Q1 interest
When used as a noun, an interest can be a hobby or activity. When used as a verb, interest can mean to attract or intrigue.

Q2 engaged
The adjective engaged can mean occupied or busy, but it can also mean promised to or pledged to be married.

Q3 novel
When used as a noun, a novel is a story or tale. When used as an adjective, novel means new or unique.

Q4 fair
The adjective fair can mean impartial or unbiased, but it can also mean fine or clear when referring to the weather.

Q5 mean
When used as a noun, mean can refer to an average or mid-point. When used as an adjective, mean means nasty or unkind.

Q6 pen
The noun pen can mean an animal enclosure or cage, but it is also a tool for writing in ink such as a ballpoint or felt-tip pen.

Q7 book
When used as a noun, a book can be a written work or volume. When used as a verb, it can mean to reserve (e.g. a table) or schedule.

Q8 kind
When used as a noun, kind can mean type or sort. When used as an adjective, it can mean caring or gentle.

Q9 lie
When used as a noun, lie can mean a falsehood or fib. When used as a verb, it can mean to recline or rest.

Q10 match
When used as a verb, match can mean to pair or unite (two things together). When used as a noun, it can mean a game (e.g. a football match) or contest.

Test 20 Related Numbers

a = the first number within the group of three

b = the third number within the group of three

Q1 54 = (a × b) + 9 = (9 × 5) + 9

Q2 8 = (a + b) ÷ 2 − 1 = (16 + 2) ÷ 2 − 1

Q3 $1 = (b \div a) \div 2 = (22 \div 11) \div 2$

Q4 $39 = (a + b) \div 2 = (31 + 47) \div 2$

Q5 $57 = (b - a) \times 3 = (34 - 15) \times 3$

Q6 $105 = a^2 + b = 9^2 + 24$

Q7 $9 = (a \div b) + 2 = (84 \div 12) + 2$

Q8 $42 = a + (b \times 3) = 24 + (6 \times 3)$

Q9 $40 = a^3 + b = 3^3 + 13$

Q10 $35 = a - b^2 = 99 - (8^2)$

Test 21 Jumbled Words with a Letter Removed

Q1   I

My uncle took me and my **SISTER** to the **FAIR** today.

Q2   N

Ben likes **WATCHING** and **PLAYING** football at the weekend.

Q3   G

The brave **KNIGHT** fought the **DRAGON** to the death.

Q4   S

Kat likes solving **ANAGRAMS** and other **PUZZLES**.

Q5   L

I'm reading a **NOVEL** about a shipwrecked **SAILOR**.

Q6   W

Yves lost his **NEW** silver **WATCH** in the park yesterday.

Q7   H

I've forgotten to **HAND** in my **HOMEWORK** again!

Q8   E

Henry **SLIPPED** and fell on the **ICE**.

Q9   M

The walkers **CLIMBED** to the **SUMMIT** then rested.

Q10   T

We have finally **BOUGHT** an **ELECTRIC** car.

Test 22 Synonyms

Q1   minute, miniscule

Q2   anguish, fret

Q3   grounded, realistic

Q4   prim, prudish

Q5   cunning, crafty

Q6   tip, gratuity

Q7   persuasive, convincing

Q8   rouse, excite

Q9   altercation, argument

Q10   house, accommodate

Test 23 Antonyms

Q1   restore, abolish

Q2   severe, lenient

Q3   melancholic, optimistic

Q4   prominent, inconspicuous

Q5   humble, superior

Q6   insufferable, appealing

Q7   giddy, steady

Q8   dynamic, sluggish

Q9   cordial, unfriendly

Q10   clandestine, obvious

Test 24 Word Combinations

Q1   hopeless (hope and less)

Q2   treetop (tree and top)

Q3   submerge (sub and merge)

Q4   turntable (turn and table)

Q5   handshake (hand and shake)

Q6   headline (head and line)

Q7   setback (set and back)

Q8   withstand (with and stand)

Q9   gatepost (gate and post)

Q10   keyboard (key and board)

Test 25 Complete the Third Pair the Same Way

Q1   camp (*delete the second letter*)

Q2   caps (*number code 1345*)

Q3   ware (*move the first letter one letter along the alphabet then change the 's' to 'r'*)

Q4   teas (*number code 4523*)

Q5   coat (*number code 1526*)

Q6   ten (*number code 423*)

Test 25 answers continue on next page

Q7 lock *(move the first letter one letter along the alphabet then remove the second letter)*

Q8 par *(number code 256)*

Q9 neon *(last two letters followed by first two letters)*

Q10 mind *(change the 'e' to 'd')*

Test 26 Missing Three-letter Words

Q1 MEN (the word in capitals is **AILMENTS**)

Q2 END (the word in capitals is **VENDING**)

Q3 ACT (the word in capitals is **REACTION**)

Q4 SEA (the word in capitals is **RESEARCH**)

Q5 EAT (the word in capitals is **SWEATY**)

Q6 ERA (the word in capitals is **OPERATIC**)

Q7 AIL (the word in capitals is **THAILAND**)

Q8 ICE (the word in capitals is **SERVICES**)

Q9 LOT (the word in capitals is **CLOTHES**)

Q10 OWN (the word in capitals is **FROWNED**)

Test 27 Code Pairs

Q1 EGGKQ (–2, –5, –8, –11, –14)

Q2 JUMPER (The code for JACKET to OMAIOO is +5, +12, –2, –2, +10, –5. So, to find the word from OGKNOM, reverse the code to –5, –12, +2, +2, –10, +5)

Q3 NLCLHS (+6, –9, –11, +5, +3, +1)

Q4 CDBZ (–5, +3, –10, +6)

Q5 HONEY (The code for GNOME to MHUGK is +6, –6, +6, –6, +6. So, to find the word from NITYE, reverse the code to –6, +6, –6, +6, –6)

Q6 BEAM (The code for WORN to DLLM is +7, –3, –6, –1. So, to find the word from IBUL, reverse the code to –7, +3, +6, +1)

Q7 ENGLISH (The code for SCIENCE to TDJFODF is each letter +1. So, to find the word from FOHMJTI, reverse the code to each letter –1)

Q8 YNUHZ (+6, –9, –10, +3, +6)

Q9 FIDFP (+3, –3, +3, –3, +3)

Q10 KVMJPRYV (–5, –9, –5, –9, –5, –9, –5, –9)

Test 28 Code Sets

Q1 3241

Q2 5241

Q3 FOOL

Q4 6423

Q5 1263

Q6 DIRT

Q7 3456

Q8 3245

Q9 PORE

Test 29 Code Sequences

Q1 HS (1st letter: –1, 2nd letter +1)

Q2 CH (1st letter: +2, +1, 0, –1, –2, 2nd letter: –2, –1, 0, +1, +2)

Q3 AZ (1st letter: –5, –3, –5, –3, –5, 2nd letter: +2, +1, 0, –1, –2)

Q4 SU (1st letter: +5, –2, +4, –1, +3, 2nd letter: –1, –2, –3, –4, –5)

Q5 PI (1st letter: +3, +2, +1, 0, –1, 2nd letter: –4)

Q6 CB (1st letter: –7, 2nd letter: +7)

Q7 KQ (1st letter: +2, –2, +1, –1, 0, 2nd letter: –2, +2, –1, +1, 0)

Q8 EB (1st letter: –1, +3, –1, +3, –1, 2nd letter: +4)

Q9 PR (1st letter: +1, +2, +3, +4, +5, 2nd letter: +2, +3, +4, +5, +6)

Q10 EW (1st letter: +1, 0, –1, –2, –3, 2nd letter: –1, –2, –3, –4, –5)

Test 30 Related Words

Q1 dessert, sandy (all the others can be synonyms for barren)

Q2 frog, turtle (all the others are mammals)

Q3 why, what (all the others can introduce a relative clause)

Q4 smooth, even (all the others are synonyms for rough)

Q5 comma, full-stop (all the others are types of sentences)

Q6 tickets, noise (all the others are types of reading material)

Q7 peace, material (all the others are synonyms for scrap)

Q8 conceal, release (all the others are synonyms for seize)

Q9 precious, wholesome (all the others are synonyms for careful)

Q10 definite, consolidated (all the others are synonyms for tentative)

Test 31 Complete the Sum

Q1 7
Q2 65
Q3 2
Q4 63
Q5 108
Q6 1
Q7 1
Q8 8
Q9 68
Q10 5

Test 32 Word Analogies

Q1 <u>cast</u>, <u>grab</u> (the words are synonyms)
Q2 <u>English</u>, <u>Dutch</u> (the words are the main languages spoken in each country)
Q3 <u>active</u>, <u>rough</u> (the words are synonyms)
Q4 <u>domestic</u>, <u>wild</u> (dogs are domestic creatures (or pets) and cheetahs are wild)
Q5 <u>triumph</u>, <u>founder</u> (the words are synonyms)
Q6 <u>cloth</u>, <u>wood</u> (a tailor works with cloth and a carpenter works with wood)
Q7 <u>signal</u>, <u>fragment</u> (the words are synonyms)
Q8 <u>link</u>, <u>rung</u> (a chain has links and a ladder has rungs)
Q9 <u>decorative</u>, <u>scruffy</u> (the words are synonyms)
Q10 <u>plants</u>, <u>planets</u> (the words describe what each original word studies; botany is the study of plants and astronomy is the study of planets)

Test 33 Letter Connections

Q1 k (flask, kerb, whisk, kite)
Q2 w (brew, wagon, sow, ward)
Q3 d (thread, dare, chord, deny)
Q4 o (halo, oven, patio, oath)
Q5 d (wield, donate, bawled, dunk)
Q6 g (gig, groan, rung, gull)
Q7 k (track, kink, link, kin)
Q8 m (calm, mode, glum, mould)
Q9 b (grub, beast, verb, bunk)
Q10 l (gruel, lather, trowel, linger)

Test 34 Hidden Words

Q1 wall (kne**w all**)
Q2 shop (i**s hop**ing)
Q3 hour (watc**h our**)
Q4 dash (looke**d ash**amed)
Q5 sang (wa**s ang**ry)
Q6 chat (flin**ch at**)
Q7 sink (pour**s ink**)
Q8 epic (th**e pic**nic)
Q9 halo (ru**sh alo**ng)
Q10 rear (The**re are**)

Test 35 Problem Solving

Q1 Chang

	Gabriel	Tilly	Jess	Chang
somersaults			✓	✓
handstands	✓			✓
backflips	✓		✓	✓
cartwheels		✓	✓	✓
trampoline		✓	✓	✓

Q2 29 + 7; 31 + 5; 17 + 19; 13 + 23

Q3 Second

Q4 They won't ever be covered.
The rungs won't ever be covered because the boat rises with the tide.

Q5 12 degrees

Belfast	Glasgow	London	Paris	Taunton
2° (same temp. as Glasgow)	2° (7° colder than London: 9 − 7 = 2)	9° (6° colder than Paris: 15 − 6 = 9)	15°	12° (3° warmer than London: 9 + 3 = 12)

Q6 South east

post office   school   N

                              W   E

          Hal's house   S

church   cinema

Test 35 answers continue on next page

Q7 **7.45 pm**

The programme and pause time last
25 + 10 minutes = 35 minutes.
7.10 pm + 35 minutes = 7.45 pm.

Q8 **3**

Gina, Freddie and Gaynor do not bring
sandwiches.

	Abdul	Cian	Gina	Freddie	Gaynor
sandwiches	✓	✓	✗	✗	✗
crisps	✓	✗	✓	✗	✗
fruit	✓	✗	✗	✓	✓
pizza	✗	✗	✗	✓	✓

Test 36 Letter Analogies

Q1 CF (1st letter +7, 2nd letter +8)

Q2 JJ (1st letter +3, 2nd letter +5)

Q3 RV (1st letter −2, 2nd letter +2)

Q4 WJ (1st letter +5, 2nd letter −13)

Q5 RA (1st letter −1, 2nd letter +5)

Q6 YZ (1st letter +2, 2nd letter +2)

Q7 NX (1st letter +11, 2nd letter +3)

Q8 IS (1st letter −5, 2nd letter +5)

Q9 RV (1st letter −4, 2nd letter −1)

Q10 SC (1st letter +3, 2nd letter +3)

Test 37 Letters for Numbers

Q1 B

Q2 E

Q3 E

Q4 D

Q5 A

Q6 E

Q7 A

Q8 B

Q9 D

Q10 B

Test 38 Number Sequences

Q1 49 (the sequence is decreasing square
numbers)

Q2 9 (the sequence is alternating even numbers
and odd numbers)

Q3 9 (the sequence is +5)

Q4 82 (the sequence is +1, +2, +3, +4, +5)

Q5 8 (this is the Fibonacci sequence: each
number is the sum of the two preceding
ones)

Q6 33 (the sequence is −15, −13, −11, −9, −7)

Q7 82 (the sequence is every other number +1
and square of every other number +1)

Q8 46 (the sequence is −9, −8, −7, −6, −5)

Q9 48 (the sequence is −12)

Q10 27 (the sequence is +3, +4, +5, +6, +7)

Test 39 Word Construction

Q1 nice (word one letter 4, word one letter 3,
word two letter 3, word two letter 4)

Q2 hake (word one letter 1, word one letter 2,
word two letter 4, word one letter 4)

Q3 reed (word one letter 3, word one letter 4,
word two letter 2, word two letter 4)

Q4 tuna (word two letter 4, word one letter 1,
word one letter 2, word two letter 2)

Q5 test (word one letter 3, word one letter 4,
word two letter 1, word two letter 2)

Q6 time (word two letter 1, word one letter 2,
word one letter 1, word one letter 4)

Q7 seam (word one letter 4, word two letter 2,
word one letter 1, word two letter 1)

Q8 rare (word two letter 2, word two letter 4,
word one letter 2, word one letter 3)

Q9 trip (word one letter 4, word one letter 3,
word two letter 2, word two letter 1)

Q10 hoop (word two letter 4, word one letter 4,
word one letter 2, word one letter 1)

Test 40 Double Meanings

Q1 **stalk**

When used as a noun, a stalk is the stem
or shoot of a plant or flower. When used
as a verb, it can mean to follow or pursue
stealthily.

Q2 **well**

When used as a noun, a well can be a hole
in the ground from which water can be
extracted, for example a waterhole or a
spring. When used as an adjective, it means
healthy and fit.

Q3 content

When used as a noun, content can mean the topic or theme (of a subject). When used as an adjective (pronounced differently), it means happy or satisfied.

Q4 firm

When used as a noun, firm means company or business. When used as an adjective, it means hard or solid.

Q5 bowl

When used as a noun, a bowl is a type of dish or basin. When used as a verb, it means to throw.

Q6 bore

The verb bore can mean to tire or exhaust (e.g. when something 'bores you to tears'), but it can also mean to drill or mine (a hole).

Q7 scale

When used as a noun, scale can refer to the degree or size of something. When used as a verb, it can mean to mount or ascend (e.g. to scale a wall).

Q8 level

When used as an adjective, level means horizontal or even. When used as a verb, it means destroy or wreck.

Q9 draw

The verb draw can mean to sketch or design, but it can also mean to pull or drag.

Q10 light

When used as a verb, light can mean illuminate or brighten. When used as an adjective, it can mean pale or fair in colour.

Test 41 Related Numbers

a = the first number within the group of three

b = the third number within the group of three

Q1 $12 = (b + 1) \div a = (143 + 1) \div 12$

Q2 $48 = (b - a) \times 4 = (69 - 57) \times 4$

Q3 $57 = a^2 - b^2 = 11^2 - 8^2$

Q4 $23 = (a \div b) - 1 = (96 \div 4) - 1$

Q5 $6 = (a \div b) \times 2 = (78 \div 26) \times 2$

Q6 $86 = (a^2 + b^2) + 1 = (36 + 49) + 1$

Q7 $192 = (a + b) \times 2 = (57 + 39) \times 2$

Q8 $26 = (a - b) \div 2 = (89 - 37) \div 2$

Q9 $153 = (a \times b) \times 3 = (17 \times 3) \times 3$

Q10 $10 = (a \div b) + 3 = (42 \div 6) + 3$

Test 42 Jumbled Words with a Letter Removed

Q1 C Ursula had rice **CAKES** with a glass of **JUICE**.

Q2 F The horse **FELL** at the **FIRST** hurdle.

Q3 O Dad placed **COAL** and **LOGS** on the fire.

Q4 Q The **QUALITY** of the food was **QUITE** poor.

Q5 A Maeve likes **SCRAMBLED** egg with **TOAST**.

Q6 V I've been **REVISING** for my **DRIVING** test all day.

Q7 N Tom is **TRAVELLING AROUND** the Greek islands.

Q8 R The **BATTERY** on my phone keeps losing its **CHARGE**.

Q9 T Mum is **CUTTING** the grass before it **STARTS** raining.

Q10 C Jen's new puppy is really **CUTE** and **CUDDLY**.

Test 43 Synonyms

Q1 nominee, candidate

Q2 recede, withdraw

Q3 loyal, faithful

Q4 misinform, mislead

Q5 meander, wind

Q6 barge, push

Q7 cultivate, grow

Q8 adhere, stick

Q9 cache, store

Q10 askew, awry

Test 44 Antonyms

Q1 appease, provoke

Q2 copious, scarce

Q3 escalate, diminish

Q4 tireless, idle

Q5 proficient, incompetent

Q6 trivial, important

Q7 squeamish, tough

Q8 painstaking, careless

Q9 reticent, frank

Q10 viscous, watery

Test 45 Word Combinations

Q1 scarecrow (<u>scare</u> and <u>crow</u>)

Q2 seafood (<u>sea</u> and <u>food</u>)

Q3 afterthought (<u>after</u> and <u>thought</u>)

Q4 showdown (<u>show</u> and <u>down</u>)

Q5 silverware (<u>silver</u> and <u>ware</u>)

Q6 broadcast (<u>broad</u> and <u>cast</u>)

Q7 trailblazer (<u>trail</u> and <u>blazer</u>)

Q8 beforehand (<u>before</u> and <u>hand</u>)

Q9 lifestyle (<u>life</u> and <u>style</u>)

Q10 freelance (<u>free</u> and <u>lance</u>)

Test 46 Complete the Third Pair the Same Way

Q1 rear (*last two letters in reverse order followed by first two letters in reverse order*)

Q2 rasp (*number code 6231*)

Q3 era (*number code 562*)

Q4 slide (*move fourth letter one letter along the alphabet*)

Q5 nest (*number code 6512*)

Q6 lug (*number code 423*)

Q7 bridal (*homophones*)

Q8 hash (*replace first two letters with the last letter*)

Q9 sat (*number code 435*)

Q10 read (*present tense, past tense*)

Test 47 Missing Three-letter Words

Q1 VAN (the word in capitals is **SERVANTS**)

Q2 FIN (the word in capitals is **FINANCES**)

Q3 RAG (the word in capitals is **DRAGON**)

Q4 TRY (the word in capitals is **PASTRY**)

Q5 ARM (the word in capitals is **WARMLY**)

Q6 INK (the word in capitals is **BLINK**)

Q7 OAR (the word in capitals is **BOARD**)

Q8 BUD (the word in capitals is **BUDDING**)

Q9 HEM (the word in capitals is **THEME**)

Q10 OUR (the word in capitals is **COLOURS**)

Test 48 Code Pairs

Q1 THFJE (−3, +3, −3, +3, −3)

Q2 SMALL (The code for HEAVY to IFBWZ is each letter +1. So, to find the word from TNBMM, reverse the code to each letter −1)

Q3 IGIQHZ (+2, −2, +3, −3, +3, −4)

Q4 FATHER (The code for MOTHER to IWTPAJ is −4, +8, 0, +8, −4, −8. So, to find the word from BITPAJ, reverse the code to +4, −8, 0, −8, +4, +8)

Q5 YJHGB (+7, +9, −1, −7, +3)

Q6 HEKKMY (−1, −2, −3, −4, −5, −6)

Q7 SMILE (The code for SULKY to HLEFV is −11, −9, −7, −5, −3. So, to find the word from HDBGB, reverse the code to +11, +9, +7, +5, +3)

Q8 BDEPE (+2, −1, +3, −2, +4)

Q9 VVQRP (−1, −13, +3, −13, −3)

Q10 TAKE (The code for GIVE to HJWF is each letter +1, So, to find the word from UBLF, reverse the code to each letter −1)

Test 49 Code Sets

Q1 6325

Q2 6213

Q3 SEAM

Q4 1234

Q5 3523

Q6 NEAR

Q7 5341

Q8 6351

Q9 NAPE

Test 50 Code Sequences

Q1 TK (1st letter: +3, −2, +3, −2, +3, 2nd letter: −3, +2, −3, +2, −3)

Q2 EL (1st letter: +3, −4, +3, −4, +3, 2nd letter: −2, −1, 0, +1, +2)

Q3 KV (1st letter: +1, +2, +1, +2, +1, 2nd letter: −2, −1, −2, −1, −2)

Q4 OM (1st letter: +5, 2nd letter −10)

Q5 NU (1st letter: +2, +4, +6, +8, +10, 2nd letter: −2, −4, −6, −8, −10)

Q6 CM (1st letter: −7, 2nd letter: +5)

Q7 NN (1st letter: +3, −1, +2, −2, +1, 2nd letter: −2, +1, −2, +2, −2)

Q8 XB (1st letter: −4, +6, +4, −6, −4, 2nd letter: +4)

Q9 PM (1st letter: +1, +2, +3, +4, +5, 2nd letter: −1, −2, −3, −4, −5)

Q10 OJ (1st letter: −4, +5, −4, +5, −4, 2nd letter: −3, −3, −3, −3, −3)

Test 51 Related Words

Q1 <u>fashionable</u>, <u>quirky</u> (all the others are synonyms for clear)

Q2 <u>Ireland</u>, <u>France</u> (all the others are continents)

Q3 <u>giddy</u>, <u>frail</u> (all the others are synonyms for ill-tempered)

Q4 <u>chest</u>, <u>finger</u> (all the others are bones)

Q5 <u>truck</u>, <u>caravan</u> (all the others are found on water)

Q6 <u>ram</u>, <u>ring</u> (all the others are names of baby animals)

Q7 <u>dish</u>, <u>cup</u> (all the others are items of cutlery)

Q8 <u>dangerous</u>, <u>disabled</u> (all the others are synonyms for dubious)

Q9 <u>concur</u>, <u>agree</u> (all the others are synonyms for conflict)

Q10 <u>run</u>, <u>flee</u> (all the others can be synonyms for fight)

Test 52 Complete the Sum

Q1 81

Q2 3

Q3 8

Q4 7

Q5 7

Q6 1

Q7 26

Q8 14

Q9 15

Q10 7

Test 53 Word Analogies

Q1 <u>fiddle</u>, <u>carpenter</u> (alternative words)

Q2 <u>hand</u>, <u>nose</u> (human equivalent of paw and snout)

Q3 <u>orchard</u>, <u>vineyard</u> (where both fruits can be grown)

Q4 <u>lose</u>, <u>release</u> (the words are antonyms)

Q5 <u>mare</u>, <u>nanny</u> (female horse and goat)

Q6 <u>flour</u>, <u>eggs</u> (the words are the main ingredients of cake and omelette)

Q7 <u>rescue</u>, <u>punish</u> (the words are synonyms)

Q8 <u>dark</u>, <u>slant</u> (the words are both fonts; bold text is darker, and with italic font the letters are slanted)

Q9 <u>badger</u>, <u>gerbil</u> (fox and badger are wild animals, while dog and gerbil are domestic pets)

Q10 <u>funny</u>, <u>ridiculous</u> (the words are synonyms)

Test 54 Letter Connections

Q1 b (lamb, benign, comb, bolt)

Q2 m (gram, maid, calm, mute)

Q3 l (wool, lend, bell, loot)

Q4 h (wrath, hind, wish, hail)

Q5 p (clasp, pint, flip, pink)

Q6 d (sped, dew, freed, dark)

Q7 y (misty, yearn, holy, yelp)

Q8 n (keen, naval, stun, nine)

Q9 d (blend, dune, maid, deluge)

Q10 m (palm, mink, groom, mood)

Test 55 Hidden Words

Q1 team (**tea m**akes)

Q2 bled (dou**ble d**are)

Q3 dove (peere**d ove**r)

Q4 shun (cra**sh un**fortunately)

Q5 real (mo**re a**lert)

Q6 very (fore**ver y**oung)

Q7 wash (**was h**er)

Q8 herb (**her b**est)

Q9 here (**her e**yes)

Q10 tint (bi**t int**erested)

Test 56 Problem Solving

Q1 Wenda

	Vita	Baz	Carl	Fay	Wenda
salt and pepper	✓	✓	✓	✓	✓
carrots					✓
parsnips					✓
leeks					✓
lentils	✓	✓	✓	✗	✓
chilli	✓	✓	✗	✗	✗
garlic	✗	✗	✓	✗	✗

Test 56 answers continue on next page

Q2 3

Luigi, Franco and Mo come by car. Eric and Maya take the bus or train. Isaac goes by bike or walks.

	Luigi	Franco	Mo	Eric	Isaac	Maya
car	✓	✓	✓			
bus				✓		✓
train				✓		✓
bike					✓	
walk					✓	

Q3 Molly

Molly only uses apples and pineapples.

	Finn	Oisìn	Joe	Molly	Becki
strawberries	✓	✗	✗	✗	✓
blueberries	✓	✗	✗	✗	✓
apples	✓	✓	✓	✓	✓
pineapples	✓	✓	✓	✓	✓
pears	✗	✓	✓	✗	✗
raspberries	✗	✗	✗	✗	✗

Q4 history and English

	Zac	Florence	Chloe	Marje	Zainab
English		✗	✗		✓
maths		✓	✓		✗
art	✓	✓	✓	✓	✓
music	✓	✗	✗	✓	✗
history					✓
PE	✓	✗	✓	✓	✓

Q5 Elsie

	Chan	Laurie	Ganesh	Ciara	Elsie
time	8 mins 45 secs	8 mins 45 secs	6 mins 25 secs	6 mins 45 secs	7 mins
position	4	4	1	2	3

Q6 3.6 kg

A	B	C	D	E
C + 1 kg = 3.6 kg	3.4 kg (same as E)	2.6 kg	3.6 kg (0.2 kg more than B)	3.4 kg

Baby C has to be the lightest because Baby A weighs 1 kg more than Baby C and we know the weights of Baby B, Baby D and Baby E.

Q7 green

	Ralf	Danny	Grainne	Sabine
green		✗		✓
blue	✗			✗
hazel		✓		✗
brown	✓		✓	✗

Q8 12

Angus is 13, Mabel is 14.

Test 57 Letter Analogies

Q1 UE (1st letter +4, 2nd letter +11)

Q2 VS (1st letter +7, 2nd letter +1)

Q3 DU (1st letter −7, 2nd letter +7)

Q4 KS (1st letter −6, 2nd letter −6)

Q5 BP (1st letter +8, 2nd letter +5)

Q6 ZY (1st letter −4, 2nd letter −6)

Q7 IO (1st letter −1, 2nd letter 0)

Q8 YL (1st letter −5, 2nd letter +3)

Q9 BJ (1st letter +6, 2nd letter −11)

Q10 AZ (1st letter −6, 2nd letter −6)

Test 58 Letters for Numbers

Q1 E

Q2 E

Q3 B

Q4 D

Q5 A

Q6 B

Q7 A

Q8 A

Q9 B

Q10 D

Test 59 Number Sequences

Q1 12 (−1, 0, +1, +2, +3)

Q2 35 (+3, +4, +5, +6, +7)

Q3 15 (square numbers −1)

Q4 31 (divide every other number by 2)

Q5 13 (prime numbers)

Q6 62 (−1, −3, −5, −7, −9)

Q7 216 (cubed numbers)

Q8 120 (×1, ×2, ×3, ×4, ×5)

Q9 270 (−30)

Q10 9 (every other number is +4 and −4)

Test 60 Word Construction

Q1 rate (word two letter 3, word two letter 2, word one letter 4, word one letter 2)

Q2 deer (word two letter 4, word one letter 4, word two letter 3, word one letter 1)

Q3 dent (word two letter 1, word one letter 2, word one letter 1, word one letter 4)

Q4 tone (word one letter 3, word two letter 2, word two letter 4, word one letter 4)

Q5 rent (word one letter 4, word one letter 2, word two letter 3, word two letter 4)

Q6 bash (word two letter 4, word one letter 2, word one letter 3, word one letter 4)

Q7 sink (word two letter 1, word one letter 2, word one letter 3, word two letter 4)

Q8 nail (word one letter 4, word one letter 3, word two letter 2, word two letter 3)

Q9 plug (word two letter 4, word two letter 1, word two letter 2, word one letter 4)

Q10 prod (word one letter 1, word one letter 4, word one letter 2, word two letter 4)

Notes

ACKNOWLEDGEMENTS

The author and publisher are grateful to the copyright holders for permission to use quoted materials and images.

Every effort has been made to trace copyright holders and obtain their permission for the use of copyright material. The author and publisher will gladly receive information enabling them to rectify any error or omission in subsequent editions. All facts are correct at time of going to press.

Published by Collins
An imprint of HarperCollins*Publishers* Limited
1 London Bridge Street
London SE1 9GF

HarperCollins*Publishers*
Macken House
39/40 Mayor Street Upper
Dublin 1
D01 C9W8
Ireland

ISBN: 978-0-00-870120-8

First published 2025

10 9 8 7 6 5 4 3 2 1

British Library Cataloguing in Publication Data.

A CIP record of this book is available from the British Library.

Author: Shelley Welsh

Publisher: Clare Souza

Project Manager: Richard Toms

Editorial: Charlotte Christensen

Cover Design: Sarah Duxbury

Text and Page Design: Ian Wrigley

Layout and Artwork: QBS

Production: Bethany Brohm

Printed in India by Multivista Global Pvt. Ltd.